BIRMINGHAM

A HISTORY IN MAPS

View of Birmingham, 1779, originally produced for The Modern Universal British Traveller *(published in 1779).*

BIRMINGHAM

A HISTORY IN MAPS

PAUL LESLIE LINE

ILLUSTRATED BY ALICJA BOROWSKA

The
History
Press

Dedicated to Mum and Dad,
and with grateful thanks to my uncle,
Peter J. Summerhayes

First published 2009
Paperback edition first published 2010

The History Press
The Mill, Brimscombe Port
Stroud, Gloucestershire, GL5 2QG
www.thehistorypress.co.uk

British Library Cataloguing in Publication Data.
A catalogue record for this book is available from the British Library.

ISBN 978 0 7524 6089 5

Typesetting and origination by The History Press
Printed in Great Britain
Manufacturing managed by Jellyfish Print Solutions Ltd

CONTENTS

View of Birmingham, 1826, engraved by Thomas Dixon.

FOREWORD

Maps both fascinate and enlighten. So many of us are drawn into scanning a map for places and streets that we know and about which we wish to learn more – and from them we are pulled into discovering other places and streets. Small-scale maps provide a wonderful overview of a town or city, providing a snapshot of its limits in a particular year and allowing comparisons over time. Large-scale maps are as vibrant, allowing us to fully grasp the overcrowding of houses and factories in working-class streets and letting us look at the openness provided by big gardens and green spaces in middle-class suburbs. Plans and surveys are also illuminating, providing us with the opportunity of almost seeing a town in 3D, or else giving us an awareness of landholding and land use.

Together maps, plans and surveys make up some of the most important sources for urban, local and family historians – and yet for all their fascination and significance they are a neglected source. Too often academic historians use them like photographs, merely for illustrative purposes. That is a mistake. The visual element of maps, plans and surveys is indeed a vital one for giving us a feel for how a town looked when there were no cameras – but there is more to be gained. They give us the information about streets, buildings and sometimes population that we would otherwise lack before the census of 1841 and the publication of regular trade directories. And even after the arrival of such valuable sources, maps remain crucial in building up a fuller picture of the nineteenth- and twentieth-century town.

View down New Street, 1836.

Maps, plans and surveys should be cherished both as key evidence in their own right and as a main source along with documentary and other sources. Together they enrich our knowledge of the past. I am, then, excited at the publication of this beautifully produced book. For the first time it brings together the leading maps, plans and surveys for eighteenth- and nineteenth-century Birmingham. With inclusions from the seventeenth and twentieth centuries, this book will become not only a delight for the general reader, but also an invaluable publication for anyone interested in researching the city's history.

Professor Carl Chinn, MBE

ACKNOWLEDGEMENTS

Many people have helped towards the compilation of this book, and indeed without the efforts of surveyors and cartographers long since laid to rest we would not be able to access the gateway to Birmingham's historic past. I would like to express my thanks to Birmingham City Archives for their permission and co-operation in making available the early plans and surveys held in their possession as a prerequisite to our own map resource at www.mapseeker.co.uk. In particular, Richard Abbott, map archivist at Birmingham Archives Services and Heritage, for his valuable research and assistance with regard to the early surveys and respective surveyors. I would like to thank Richard Albutt and his team at Birmingham Central Library Digital Laboratory for the professional scanning of original surveys ready for artwork. This brings me to Alicja Borowska, who has spent many hours adding a new dimension to the early plans and surveys of Birmingham, meticulously transforming them from their original black and white into colour. I would like to add a special thanks to Collins Bartholomew Ltd for allowing the reproduction of the AA Throughway Map of Birmingham from the Collins Bartholomew Archive and in particular to Kathryn Kelly, Cartographic Services Manager and David Jamieson, Information Archivist and Map Librarian at Harper Collins. Grateful acknowledgement is also made to Gil and Gem Wilyman of Heritage for their kind permission to include many images of Birmingham from bygone years from their collection that have added a valuable pictorial dimension to both the accompanying history and map resource. Many thanks also to Steve Bartrick for his efforts in obtaining additional pictorial resources to accompany the many maps, plans and surveys. Special thanks to Sue Stokes for her support in the compilation of the accompanying text, and my partner Jan, without whose aid this volume could not have been completed. This brings me to the present and the future; a special acknowledgement to Jim Wilson and the City Centre Development Team for permission to include material for the future vision of Birmingham and sharing their plans and ideas in the many projects underway within the 'Big City Plan' for Birmingham.

BLUE COAT
SCHOOL

INTRODUCTION

From *Beormingham*, one of many market towns in the Hemlingford Hundred, as described on Saxon's fourteenth-century county map of Warwickshire, to *Birmingham*, now our nation's second largest city, this volume aims to reveal through rare maps and town plans how Birmingham became the birthplace of manufacturing, the powerhouse of the industrial revolution, and, at one stage in its history, the toyshop capital of Europe.

The maps, plans and surveys featured in this volume, some recreated in colour for the first time, open a visual gateway to each historic chapter in Birmingham's history, collectively painting a portrait of that fascinating journey through time. The creators of these archives could never imagine how important their hard work would become; treasures amongst our rich and historical national heritage.

Accompanying these plans and surveys are many antique illustrations that have been restored, cleaned and enhanced. They include interesting town views, vistas down some of the city's oldest streets, as well as a selection of Birmingham's important and well-known buildings, many long since gone. There are also some trade plates from the nineteenth century, completing the pictorial dimension.

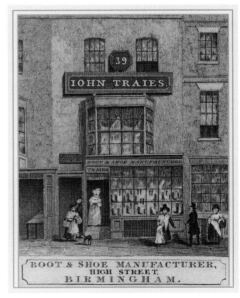

Many hours of painstaking work and specialist contribution have brought this collection together, reproducing directly from the original archive and enabling every intricate detail to be captured. Without the technology of today, I cannot imagine how we would have achieved completion of this volume. This fact alone makes me ponder how the cartographers, surveyors, engravers and publishers of yesteryear achieved such detailed work, and in a lot of cases 'works of art', all those centuries ago.

Many history books on Birmingham have been written through the centuries, each with a unique content, style and focus. The objective of this project has been to present and bring together at the most detailed level, here in one publication, Birmingham's principal historic plans and surveys.

Birmingham's most important old plans and surveys follow this introduction, highlighting key events in Birmingham's transition from market town to industrial city. The author hopes that, with this comprehensive resource at your fingertips, you will enjoy exploring Birmingham's incredible journey.

Paul Leslie Line, 2009

One
THE MANOR LOST

At the time of the first detailed survey, carried out by the Crown to evaluate its newly acquired possession, Birmingham was already a prosperous market town. It is left to our conjecture how it was Birmingham, rather than any neighbouring hamlet or village, which had developed by this time into a prosperous market town.

View of Birmingham, 1640.

The conjectural plan of Birmingham was compiled by Joseph Hill (1835-1914), a prominent Birmingham antiquarian of the late nineteenth and early twentieth centuries. It was based largely on the survey of Birmingham made by the Crown in 1553 (hence the date on the map). The plan accompanied the printed transcript of this survey. The survey was translated from the Latin by W.B. Bickley, with notes and introduction by Joseph Hill, and was first published in 1890. The full survey has the title:

> Survey of the Borough of Birmingham and the Manor and Lordship of the Foreign of Birmyncham, in the County of Warwick, part of the possessions of John, late Duke of Northumberland, attainted of high treason, and formerly part of the possessions of Edward Birmyncham, attainted of felony.

In 1536 John Dudley, later Duke of Northumberland, gained ownership of the Manor of Birmingham after falsely accusing Edward Birmyncham, last in a line of Norman barons, of highway robbery.

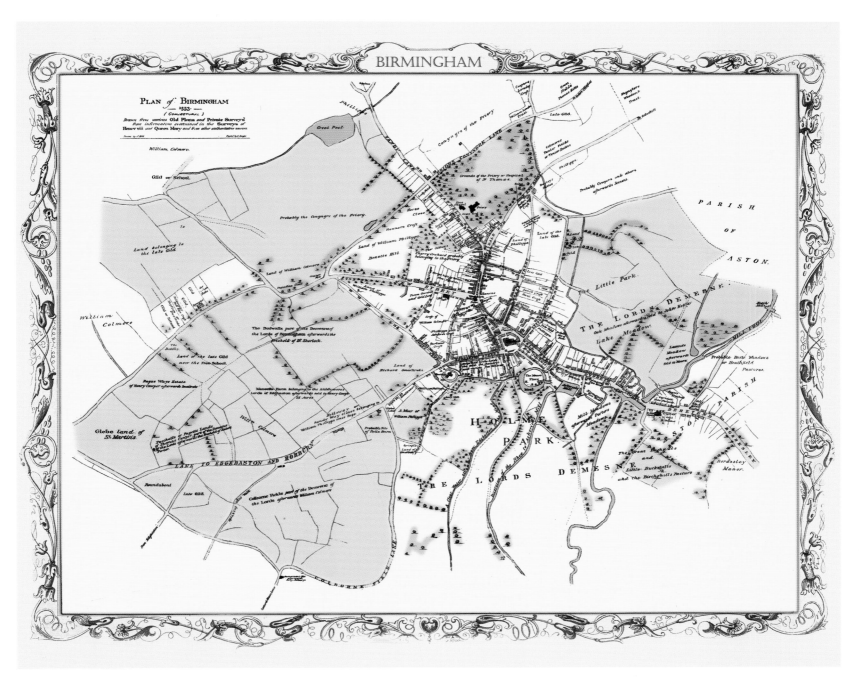

Joseph Hill's conjectural plan of Birmingham, 1553.

As they say, what goes around comes around. The Manor of Birmingham was forfeited to the Crown in 1553 following the unsuccessful attempt by John Dudley, Duke of Northumberland, to make his son's wife, Lady Jane Grey, Queen of England following the death of Edward VI. When Mary I became Queen, Northumberland was found guilty of high treason and executed.

So it is then that their unfortunate demise had such an influence on the subsequent development of Birmingham. Also, with Henry VIII's dissolution of the monasteries and religious guilds, the Priory Hospital in 1536 and the Guild of the Holy Cross in 1547, large areas of land became available, sold and released for development. However, the rapid development and increase in industry did not come until a half century later. Throughout the sixteenth century, and indeed much later, the ancient parish remained rural in character.

At the time of the survey it was clear that in terms of Birmingham's major industry, the transition from cloth, wool and leather to metal-based industries had already taken place.

In 1538, John Leland, the Tudor historian, thus described Birmingham:

> The beauty of Birmingham, a good market town in the extreme parts of Warwickshire, is one good street going up along, almost from the left ripe [shore] of the brook up a meane [small] hill by the length of a quarter of a mile. I saw but one parish church in the town. There be many smiths in the town that used to make knives and all manner of cutting tools, and many lorimers that make bitts, and a great many naylors, so that a great part of the town is maintained by smiths, who have their iron and coal out of Staffordshire.

From the surveys of 1553 and Hill's conjectural plan based on them, houses, both domestic tenements and public buildings, abutted on the main High Street and the roads led off it east and west.

There were few buildings along New Street; the Guild Hall, being the 'Guild of the Holy Cross', founded back in 1392, is clearly marked. Its land and building were confiscated as part of the dissolution of monasteries in 1547. However, in 1552 King Edward VI returned to the town some of the plundered property from the reformation, turning the old Guild Hall into a grammar school, namely King Edward VI Grammar School; the charter of the 'free Grammer Schole' of King Edward VI was issued on 2 January 1552.

The Priory of St Thomas, demolished in 1547, and its extensive lands containing many large trees and an ancient cemetery are well marked on Hill's conjectural map; the land today is now bounded by Bull Street, Dale End, Stafford Street and Steelhouse Lane. St John's Chapel, Deritend, was then surrounded by trees, and a little further on an enclosure (marked on the survey as the Great Buckstalls and Little Buckstalls, and the Birchhills Pastures) is today the site of Birchall Street.

Due to conflicting estimates for the population, and the number of houses at the time of the survey, it is fair to assume that there were less than 200 households and a population of around 1,400, far less than the neighbouring towns. However, in the next 200 years the boundaries would remain identical but almost the whole area would be covered with buildings.

St Martin's Church, 1640.

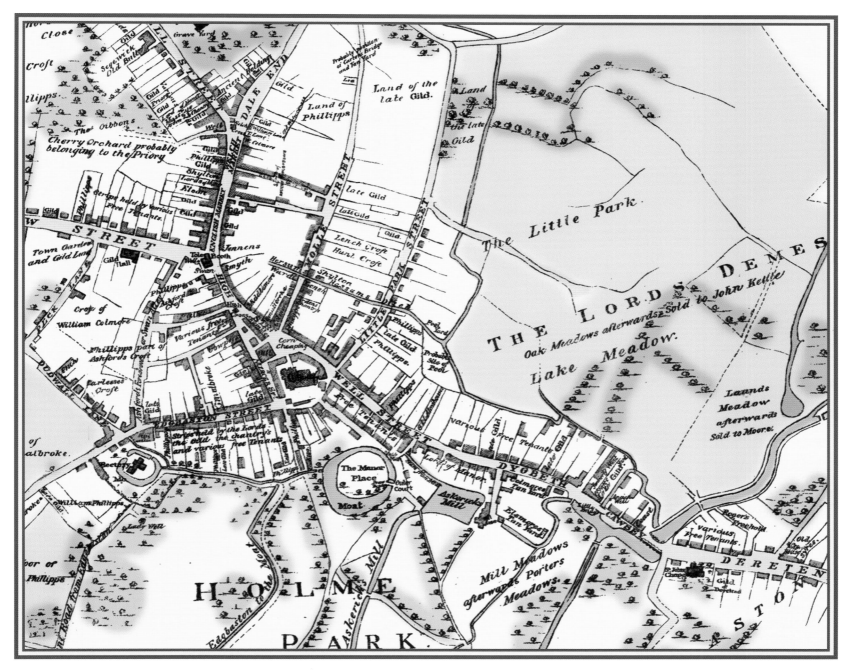

Joseph Hill's conjectural plan of Birmingham, 1553. (Middle segment)

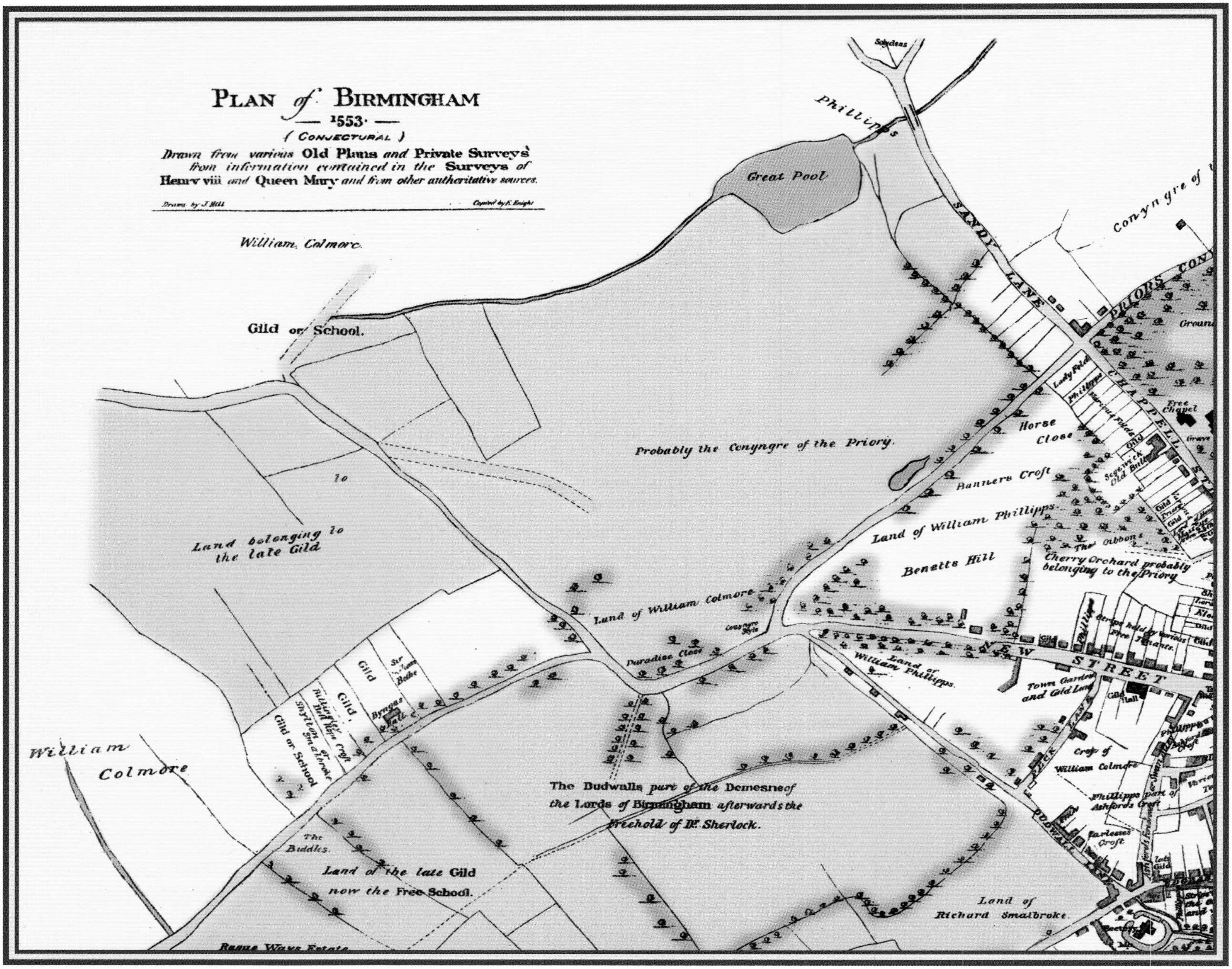

PLAN of BIRMINGHAM
— 1553. —
(CONJECTURAL)
Drawn from various Old Plans and Private Surveys
from information contained in the Surveys of
Henry viii and Queen Mary and from other authoritative sources.

Drawn by J Hill   *Copied by E Knight*

Joseph Hill's conjectural plan of Birmingham, 1553. (Top left segment)

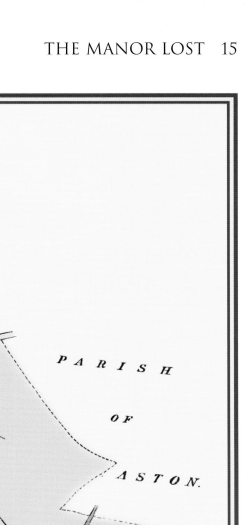

Joseph Hill's conjectural plan of Birmingham, 1553. (Top right segment)

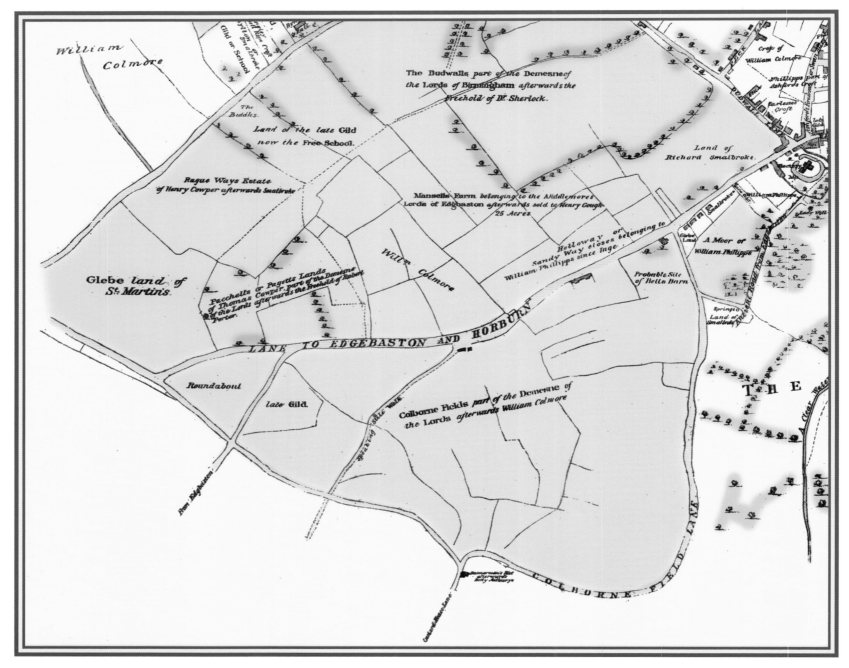

Joseph Hill's conjectural plan of Birmingham, 1553. (Bottom left segment)

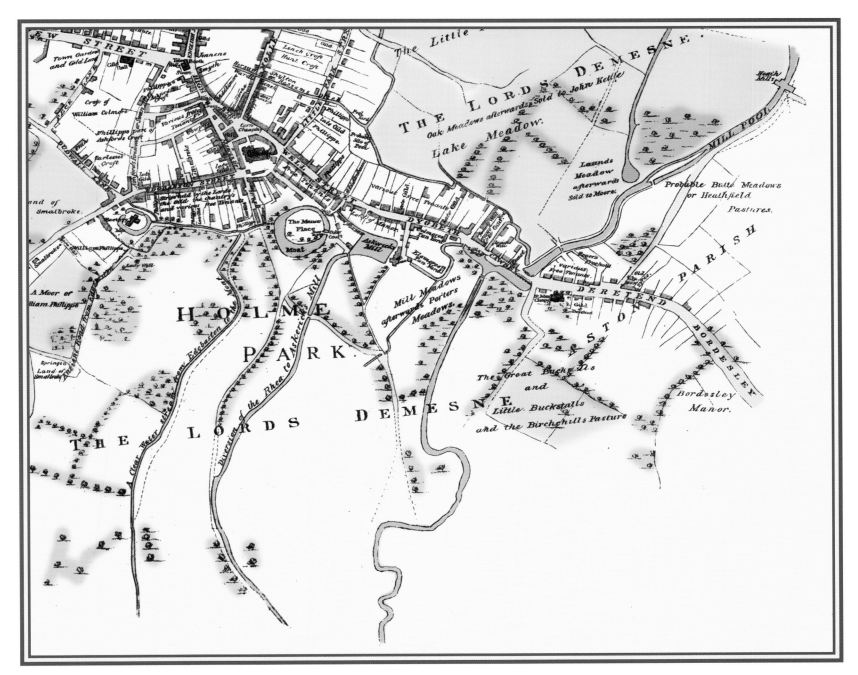

Joseph Hill's conjectural plan of Birmingham, 1553. (Bottom right segment)

Two
THE 'ANONYMOUS' COUNTY MAP

Prior to 1579, Britain's cartographic representation had been limited to general maps of not very great detail or accuracy and just a handful of town plans, including London and Cambridge. Recognising the lack of adequate maps for home defence and for local use, Sir Thomas Seckford, a Master of Requests in Queen Elizabeth's Court, commissioned Christopher Saxton, a Cheshire man, to survey and have published a series of maps of England and Wales. Saxton is credited with much of the mapping himself and the maps were finely engraved by a group of English and Flemish artisans, and were published in London. The maps were first published in finished atlas form in 1579 and the copperplates remained usable and were re-published over the next 150 years.

The 'anonymous' county map of Warwickshire, part of the Birmingham Archives Collection, was the first map to show roads and the boundaries of the hundreds. It was one of a series of twelve 'anonymous' county maps dated 1602 or 1603, attributed to William Smith, antiquary and herald. The earliest version of the Warwickshire map carried no publisher's name, but another map in the same series bears the imprint of Hans Woutneel, a Dutch bookseller resident in London between around 1584 and 1604; at least some of the maps may have been produced in Amsterdam.

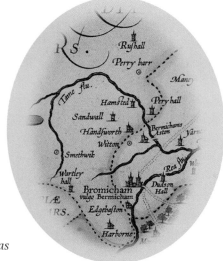

Section of the 1603 'anonymous' county map showing Birmingham as 'Bromicham'.

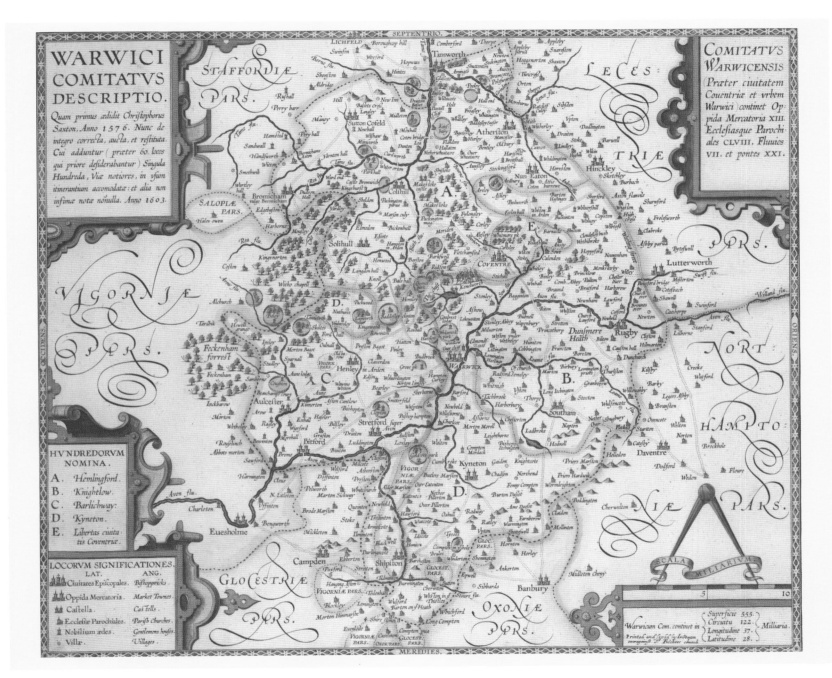

The 'anonymous' county map of Warwickshire, 1603.

Roughly translated from the Latin, the descriptions at the top left and top right respectively read:

Description of the County of Warwick which was first compiled by Christopher Saxton in the year 1576, now completely corrected, with additions, and redrawn; to which have been added (besides 60 places which were previously omitted) individual hundreds, the principal roads suitable for use by travellers and several other [features] of not inconsiderable importance, [published] in the year 1603.

The county of Warwick includes, besides the city of Coventry and the town of Warwick, XIII (13) market towns, CLVIII (158) parish churches, VII (7) rivers and XXI (21) bridges.

The hundreds were administrative subdivisions of counties in Anglo-Saxon England, and had existed since the tenth century. The names of the hundreds originated from the hundred meeting place where many of the judicial activities were carried out, in many cases remote from any settlement. Birmingham was in Hemlingford Hundred – Hemlingford, until replaced by a bridge, was a ford over the River Tame near Kingsbury.

The thirteen market towns that include Birmingham, (marked as *Bromicham* and *Bermicham*) are identified on the map by individual castle-shaped red buildings that give the false impression that they were, at the time, of equal size, with the town of Warwick and the city of Coventry next in size and importance respectfully. However, at the time the map was published around 1603, Birmingham's population was well over 2,000 and over the next fifty years the population would more than double to around 5,000, overtaking Warwick in size, and second only to Coventry. Aston is marked as *Bermichams Aston*, further illustrating Birmingham's growing importance.

In 1607, Saxton's maps formed the basis for a series of maps engraved by William Kip and William Hole to illustrate William Camden's *Britannia: An Historical Guide to the Country*.

Potential factors in Birmingham's developing importance were the early market charter (*c.* 1154), the lax controls associated with absentee landlords following the end of a long line of resident landlords, the close proximity of the town to iron and coalfields and the adaptability of the workforce to work with a variety of small products, requiring a high level of skill.

During the Civil War (1641-1651), Birmingham supplied arms to Parliament's cause. As a result of the anti-Royalist stance of the townspeople, Birmingham was assaulted and pillaged by a Royalist army under the command of Prince Rupert. Estimates of over eighty

Aston Hall.

houses were burnt down in the process. At the end of the Civil War Birmingham's manufacture of a multitude of metal-based products continued apace. The town was able to capitalise on the misfortune of London's industries, which had been significantly disrupted by the Great Fire of London (1666) and outbreak of bubonic plague. Little is known about how many people in Birmingham perished due to this terrible disease. Records show that around 500 people died in neighbouring Coventry, and testimony to those who perished in Birmingham can be seen in the early plans of Birmingham, at a place called Pest's Field, where the dead were buried, at that time well outside the town.

Despite the growing population, the built-up area of the town was not extended appreciably until the last quarter of the seventeenth century; the increasing population was accommodated within the old streets, some of which became badly congested with small properties, especially in Digbeth and Deritend. The hearth tax returns for 1670, 1673 and 1683 record no new houses in Deritend in those years, which suggest that saturation point had most likely been reached in that district. During the last quarter of the seventeenth century wealthier classes, including successful iron merchants, began moving out of the built-up town centre, leaving their large houses (many with extensive gardens and courtyards) and enabling speculative builders to develop many tenements.

Such activities at this time suggest that a population explosion was occurring in Birmingham. This is somewhat substantiated by the rise in baptisms recorded in the register of St Martin's, rising from seventy in 1680 to 210 in 1685.

As a new century approached, three factors would contribute to the steady growth of the town in the eighteenth century.

In Birmingham there had been few guilds, hence fewer restrictions on setting up new businesses in the wide-ranging industries that were starting to flourish.

Many dissenters, with freedom to pursue their own beliefs, moved to Birmingham because of the relative freedom to worship at a time when the Church of England was strictly the official church. These were to include Quaker, Baptist, Methodist, Episcopalian and Presbyterian, pre-empting the construction of many new Meeting Houses on subsequent surveys.

The growing influence and the number of Birmingham toymakers would soon play a significant part in the growth of the town; toys were not necessarily for children, back then 'toys' was a descriptive reference for a range of small metal goods including buttons, buckles and snuffboxes, among other things.

The town's infrastructure was bulging, and land for building and conversion was at a premium. The size and shape of Birmingham and its surrounding area was about to start changing beyond all expectation.

Old Meeting House.

Three
A NEW CHURCH WITH A VIEW

William Westley's plan was not drawn as all the other plans illustrated in this book. Instead it had west at the top of the map, rather than the north. However, despite this anomaly, he is credited not only in creating the first ever plan of Birmingham, but also for his skills as a carpenter and surveyor/architect. Westley's Row on the Priory Estate is named after him, as he is generally acknowledged as being the designer of the Priory Estate – the first 'planned estate' in Birmingham. William Westley, it seems, had a strong association with St Philip's Church. He is also likely to have been the architect responsible for Temple Row; three-storey houses overlooking St Philip's – the very church for which he had contributed his skills by laying wooden floors and erecting the gallery during its completion in 1715.

The plan shows the remaining buildings of the former Manor House on an oval island, about 126 yards long by 70 yards at its widest, surrounded by a moat about 12 yards broad. A stream connects the moat around the parsonage of St Martin's.

Paradise Street, now in the core area of our city centre, was then but a road through fields, yet many years later became the location of the Town Hall. The plan shows there were still cherry orchards present, between New Street and Bull Street. The open space

St Philip's Church.

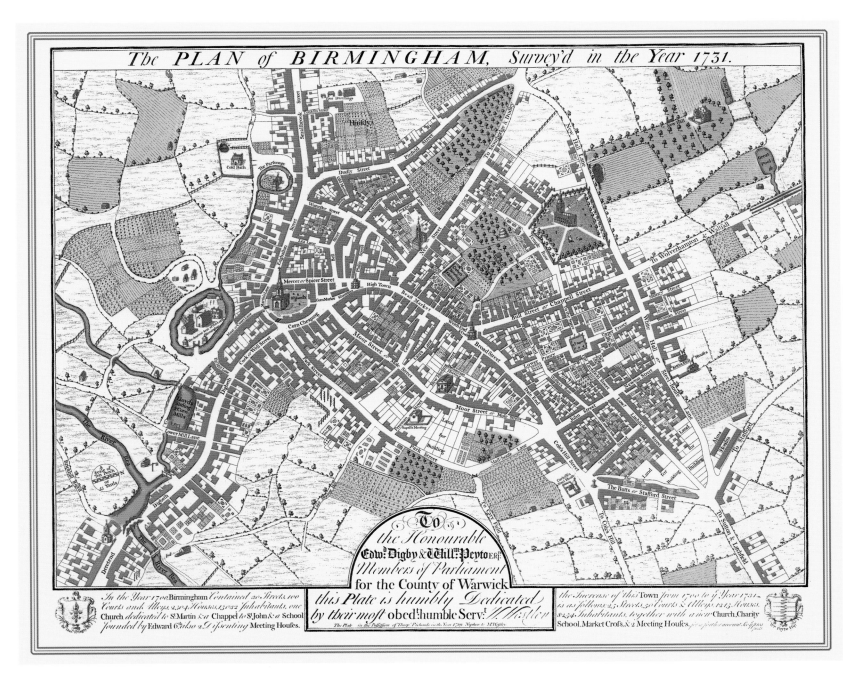

William Westley's plan of Birmingham, 1731.

next to St Martin's is marked as the corn market. Birmingham had acquired another school, called the Blue Coat School, built in 1724 as a charity school for boys and girls, which was situated on New Hall Lane and later re-named Colmore Row.

By the time of Westley's plan, the piecemeal development of the existing built-up area of the town, along with the construction of new streets, was well underway. The first of these streets, Philip Street, Colmore Street and Bell Street, were constructed with fine houses, boasting a high quality of construction on land below Peck Lane and were completed in the final decade of the seventeenth century. Philip Street and Bell Street were named after land/property owners Robert Philip and William Bell. Colmore Street was laid through School Croft, leased from William Colmore. These houses, built for the skilled artisans of the growing town, marked the period in which house construction changed from timber frame to brick in Birmingham.

In the thirty years from the turn of the century to 1731, Birmingham would grow almost half again in size. Westley gives us this information in his survey. He states that the number of Birmingham Streets had increased from thirty to fifty-five, courts and alleys from 100 to 150 and houses from 2,504 to 3,756. Based on his statistics, the population had grown from 15,032 in 1700 to 20,286 in 1731. However, this is only an estimate based on the number of persons living in houses.

The Priory Estate was built on the lands of the Priory of St Thomas. After acquiring the land from 1697, John Pemberton, a Quaker ironmonger, started to lay out the estate for development and conveying plots to developers soon after completing his purchase. Pemberton had purchased the land off the Smallbrooke family, who had previously purchased the land from the Holte family, who came into possession of the land following the priory's suppression in 1547.

With a central 'square', houses built on this estate were to be of a standard fit only for the mixture of gentry and successful industrialists. This level of occupancy was upheld with a number of agreements; these included forbidding the letting of buildings to butchers or smiths. By 1722 the estate had been completed.

On 23 May 1709 the church commissioners first met at the Swann Inn to discuss the building of a new church. The building of St Philip's commenced on 4 acres of land named Horse Close, on the brow of a hill overlooking St Martin's and the old town.

Soon after completion in 1715, you could have admired the view from one side of the churchyard across New Hall Street, later named Colmore Row. With ground sloping down before you, looking out to your left you would see Summer Hill, New Hall Hill and Ludgate Hill; to the right Snow Hill, with Constitution Hill just behind. They were gently rolling hills and pasture land, from which, on a clear day, you could see the villages of Handsworth and Aston with Barr Beacon in the distance. There were attended fields, woods and ponds, the largest of which, the Great Pond, was a little over to the right at the bottom of Snow Hill.

Swan Hotel, High Street, Birmingham.

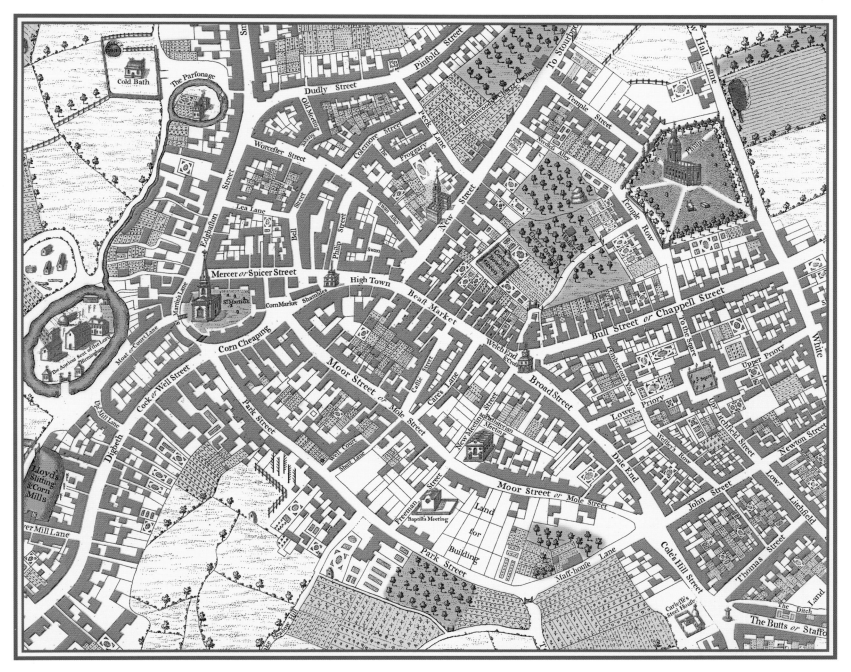

William Westley's plan of Birmingham, 1731. (Middle segment)

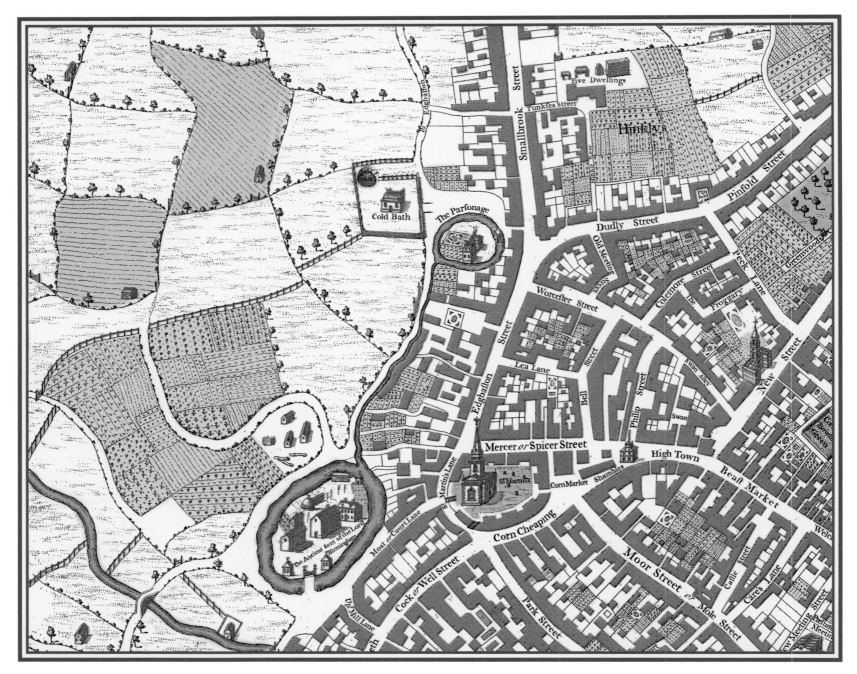

William Westley's plan of Birmingham, 1731. (Top left segment)

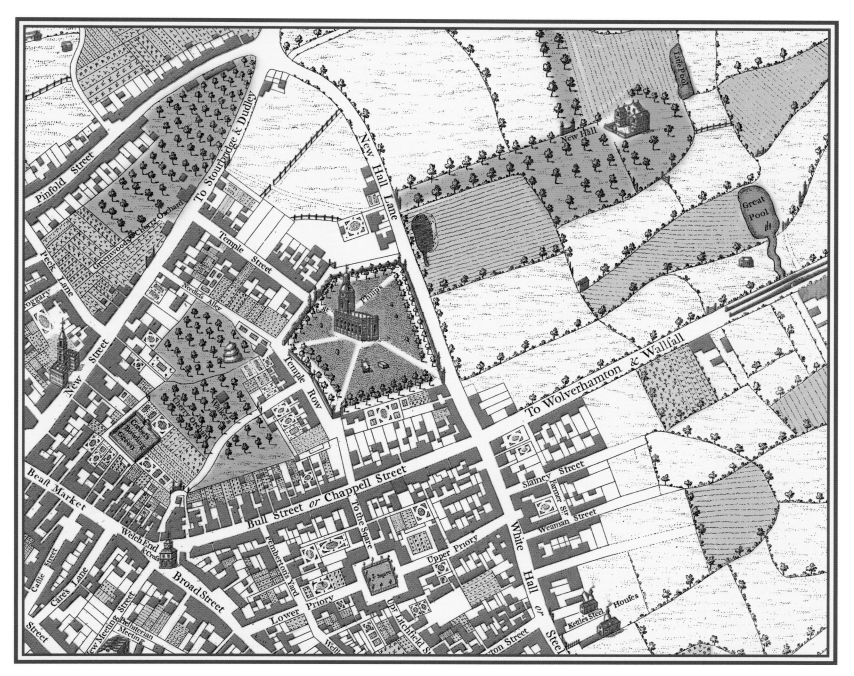

William Westley's plan of Birmingham, 1731. (Top right segment)

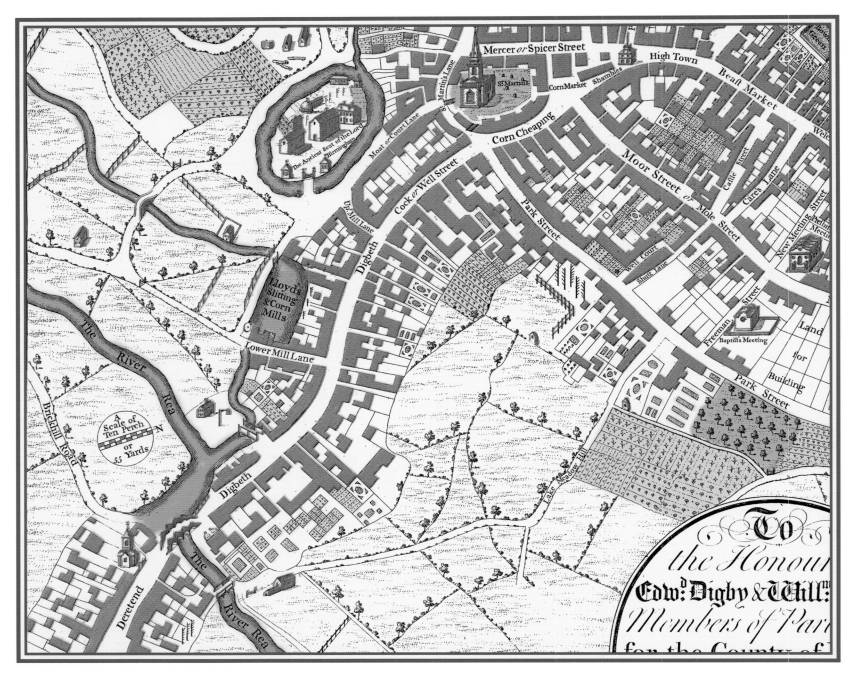

William Westley's plan of Birmingham, 1731. (Bottom left segment)

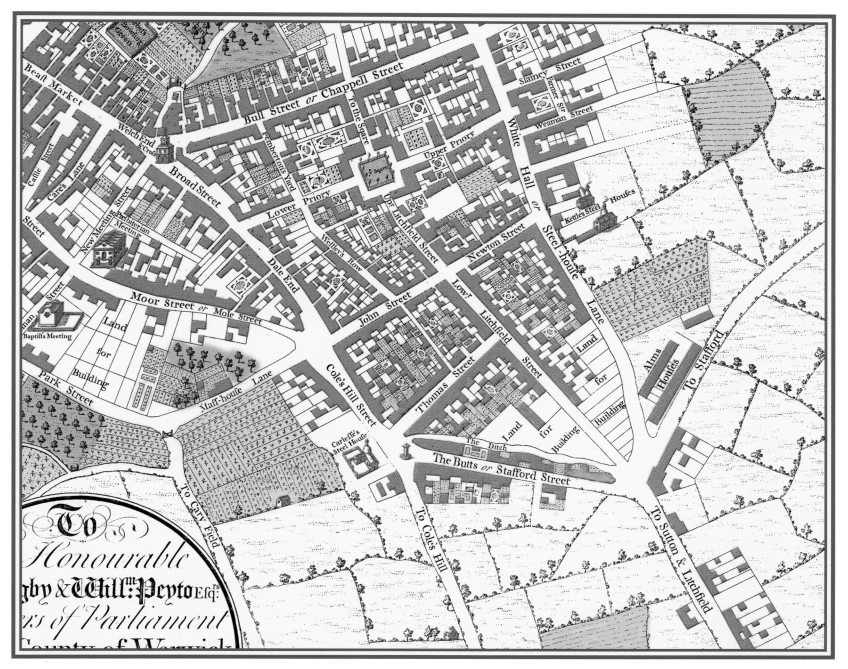

William Westley's plan of Birmingham, 1731. (Bottom right segment)

Four
MARKETS AND TOYMAKERS

Samuel Bradford, the son of Henry Bradford, a Quaker timber merchant, was born on 11 April 1725 and later became a surveyor. Land along what was to become Bradford Street, on the other side of the River Rea crossing at Deritend, was donated later by his father to anyone willing to establish a trade there.

The old workhouse, Lichfield Street, 1733-1853.

The survey's orientation has north at the top; many landmarks are named. The plan of 1750 was produced with a scale of four chains to one inch. There are even separate symbols for deciduous trees and conifers.

There is a list of the streets and lanes, with the number of houses and inhabitants in each. The town had grown steadily since Westley's map almost twenty years earlier. There were several new streets in the area to the north-west of St Philip's, already quite built up; Colmore Row is now featured for the first time, replacing New Hall Lane. Behind Colmore Row, named after the famous Colmore family that had resided for generations at New Hall, Charles Street, is just one of a number of streets being laid out for building. New Hall appears on this plan in its separate grandeur for the last time, with Newport Street running up its former access driveway. The top end of New Street, then named Swinford Street, is still bounded on both sides with land not yet built on. Several areas are marked as 'Land for Building', with plots marked out in the streets to the west and north-west of St Philip's, and to the north-east of the city centre.

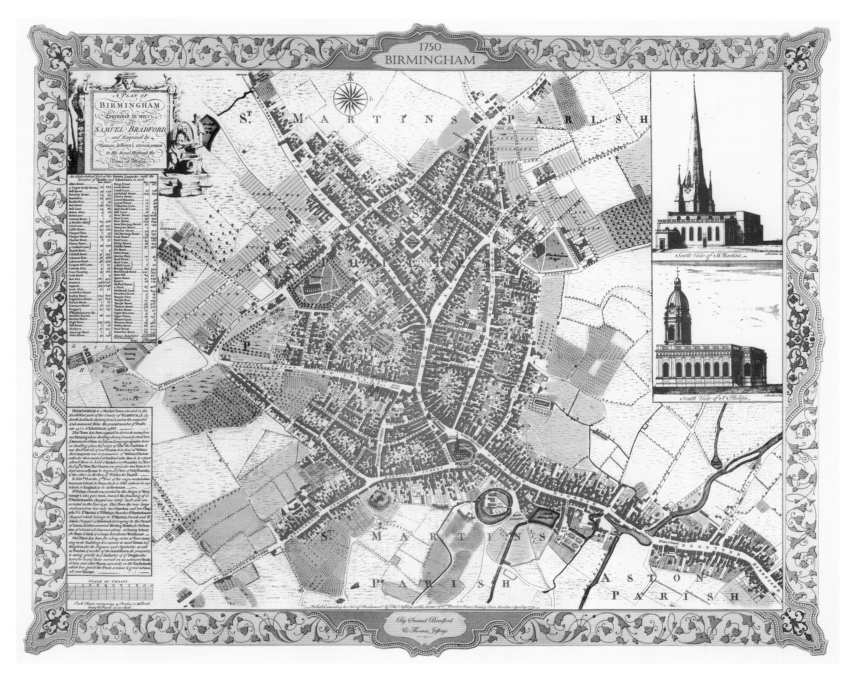

Plan of Birmingham, surveyed in 1750 by Samuel Bradford and engraved by Thomas Jefferys.

Two key buildings of note appear on the plan of 1751. St Bartholomew's Chapel was built in 1749 to serve the area expanding to the east of the town. Lichfield Street Workhouse was erected around 1734 at a cost of £1,173 3s 5d. On the plan it is situated at the lower end of Lichfield Street, now part of Corporation Street; it stood on a site that is today occupied by the Victoria Law Courts.

The recreational sport of bowls seems to have continued, with Packwood's Green at the back of High Street and Merridith's Green to the far left of the plan.

As the town grew, the markets at its very core continued to flourish. The streets were alive with people trading in all manner of goods. The plan is sufficient in detail to show the market crosses at the two extremities of High Street; the Welsh Cross, denoting the site of the Welsh market, and the Old Cross on the site of the English market, with the 'shambles' clearly marked. The corn market is clearly shown on the plan of 1750 in the open space in front of St Martin's Church, with the 'swine market' located at the High Street end of New Street. There were indeed other market products in competition for the limited space, and strict rules seem to have been in place to maintain the separate market identities. In 1749 the sellers of earthenware and garden produce were warned not to encroach upon the open space reserved for the corn market. The cheese market was moved to the Welsh Cross in 1768. Other markets would join the competition as the century progressed.

However, Birmingham's market traders were not the only people whose trade was increasing. In *England's Gazetteer*, published about this date, Birmingham, or Bromichan as it was then known, is said to be 'a large, well-built and populous town, noted for the most ingenious artificers in boxes, buckles, buttons, and other iron and steel ware.'

By now Birmingham's toymakers were well established and known throughout Europe for their wide variety of small, and often quite elaborate artefacts, made in a wide variety of precious metals, ivory and tortoise shells.

One of these toymakers, whose business close to his house in Snow Hill had flourished in the first half of the century, was Matthew Boulton, producer of buckles and buttons. At this time he had just taken his son, Matthew Boulton Junior, into the business after he had completed his education at St Johns, Deritend. Later, Matthew Boulton Junior, like John Taylor, another famous toymaker before him, would pioneer the mass production of toys. However, his abilities as an entrepreneur and world-famous industrialist would even later have the most profound impact on our town. Towards the end of the century, Birmingham would be described as the 'First Manufacturing Town in the World', the epicentre of the Industrial Revolution, exploding the growth of this once medieval town with Anglo-Saxon beginnings.

The Welsh Cross (left), demolished in March 1803, and the Old Cross (right), demolished in August 1784.

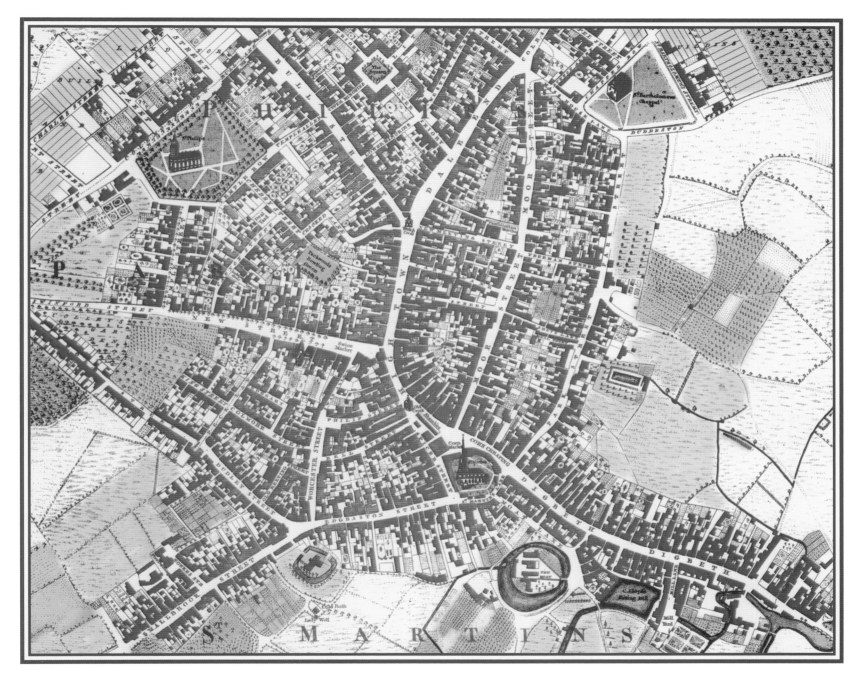

Plan of Birmingham, surveyed in 1750 by Samuel Bradford and engraved by Thomas Jefferys. (Middle segment)

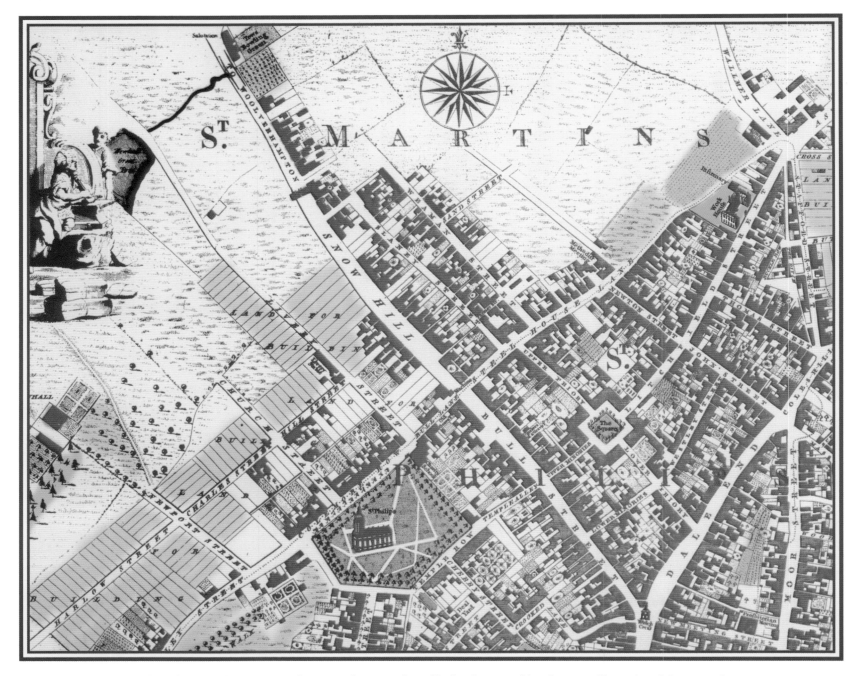

Plan of Birmingham, surveyed in 1750 by Samuel Bradford and engraved by Thomas Jefferys. (Top left segment)

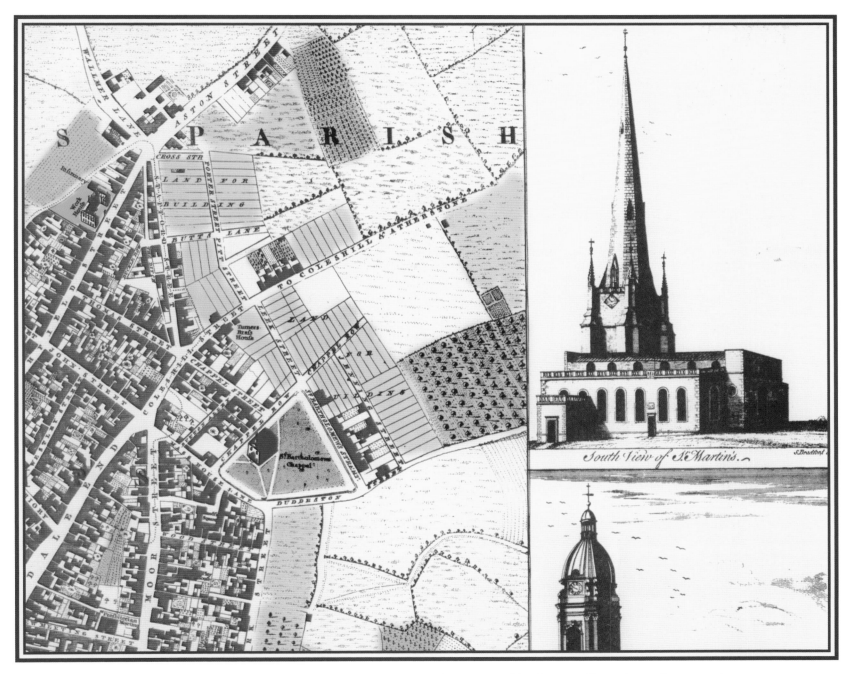

Plan of Birmingham, surveyed in 1750 by Samuel Bradford and engraved by Thomas Jefferys. (Top right segment)

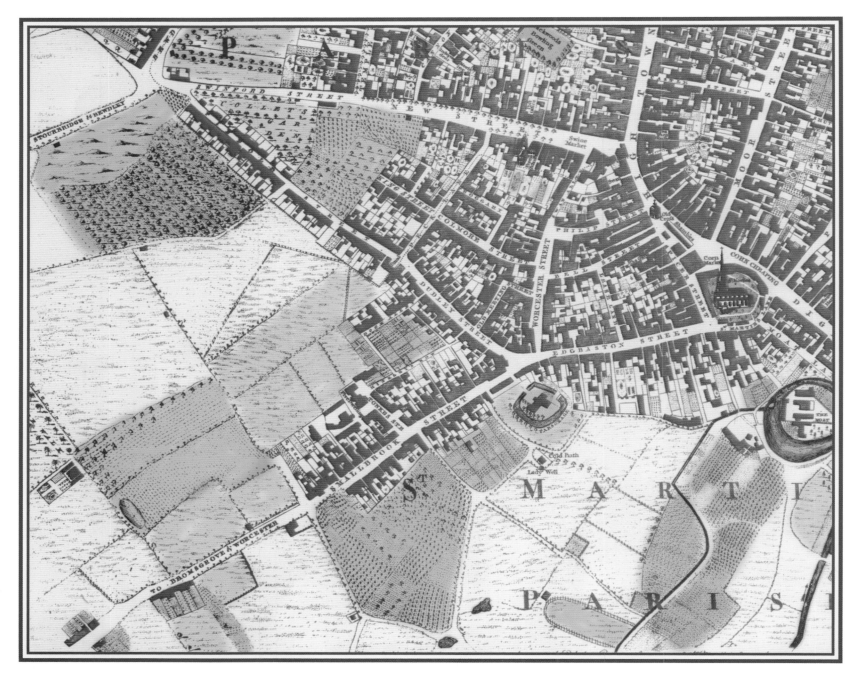

Plan of Birmingham, surveyed in 1750 by Samuel Bradford and engraved by Thomas Jefferys. (Bottom left segment)

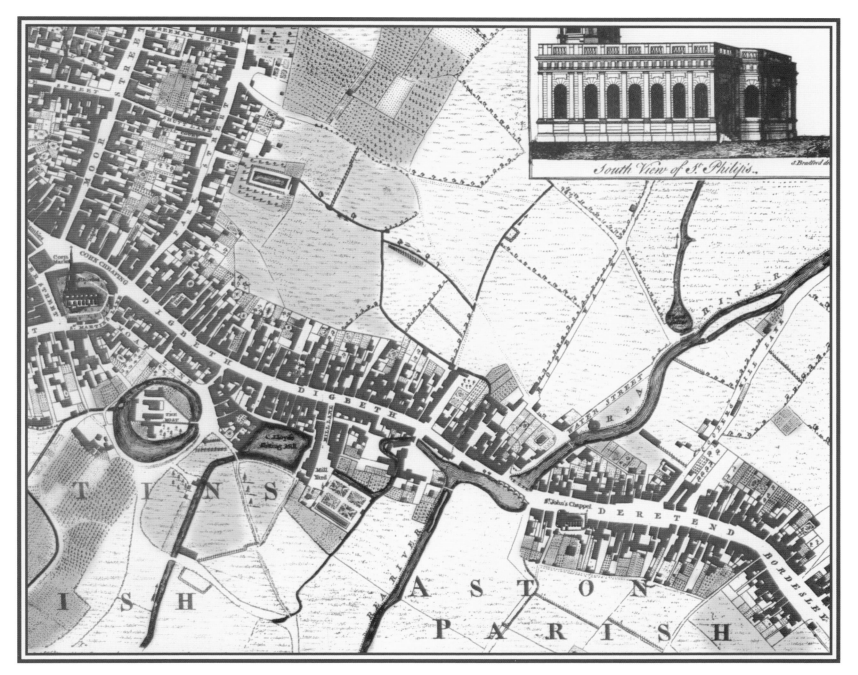

Plan of Birmingham, surveyed in 1750 by Samuel Bradford and engraved by Thomas Jefferys. (Top right segment)

Five
CANAL MANIA

Almost thirty years after Samuel Bradford's survey of 1750, Hanson's survey of 1778 clearly shows that a street pattern very similar to that of today was beginning to emerge. Buildings had now spread from Colmore Row as far out as the new church of St Paul's, built to serve the growing population and designed by Roger Eykyn of Wolverhampton. Hanson's survey is adorned with illustrations of key buildings.

The Canal Office.

At the bottom right, Henry Bradford's emerging Warner Fields estate is featured, stretching from the River Rea to Bordesley. Bradford Street ends at the river; the watercourse not only represented a physical barrier but also marked the limit of the estate and the parish boundary with Aston.

At the top, Birmingham's long-awaited hospital is shown. However, the establishment would not open in Summer Lane until 1779, as building work had not recommenced until as late as 1777. Work on the hospital building had started back in 1766, and then later that same year it was suspended due to lack of funding. At the time of Dr Ash's proposal for a hospital back in 1765, with factory and mine owners realising the value of water transport, potential investors diverted their attention elsewhere. The 'Canal Age', although short, would be responsible for opening up Britain to the Industrial Revolution. Hanson's survey heralds the arrival of the canals in Birmingham. The town's thriving industry is now connected with the coal mines of the Black Country as well as the Staffordshire and Worcester Canal via Tipton, Bilston and Smethwick.

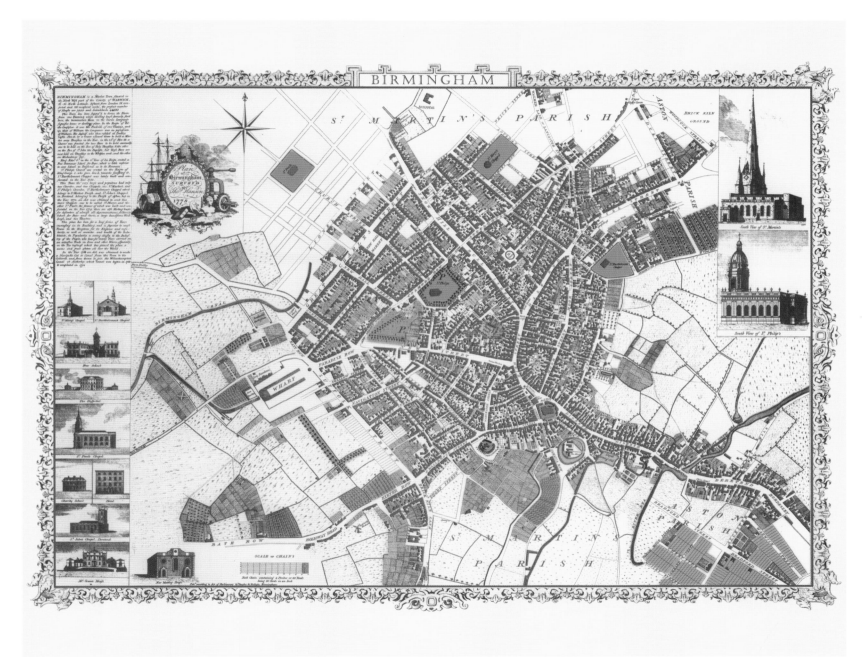

Plan of Birmingham, surveyed by Thomas Hanson, 1778.

Work started on the canal in March 1768, and with all involved working at a phenomenal rate, the stretch from the coal mines at Wednesbury to Paradise Street was in operation by the end of 1769. The latter stages of the project were not so brisk. The Birmingham canal terminus was reached at New Hall Street in 1771; a year later the connecting locks at Wolverhampton were completed, joining the canal with Staffordshire and Worcester. Although Brindley had submitted proposals based on his survey, engineers Samuel Simcock and Robert Whitworth were in charge. James Brindley was involved in the construction of six canals at the time and just could not undertake the day-to-day supervision. Yet despite his noted absence, his name connects the city's heritage with the many unsung pioneers of the canal age, the vibrant leisure and business destination of today – Brindley Place.

Hanson's survey not only features the dawn of the canal age, but also for the first time records the place name on his survey that almost everyone now associates with Birmingham: the Bull Ring, marked in the open market space in front of St Martin's. The area up to now had been referred to as Corn Cheaping in reference to the corn market on the site, also marked.

King Edward VI Grammar School, 1829.

The name Bull Ring referred to the green within Corn Cheaping to which bulls were tied for baiting before slaughter. In 1782 William Hutton recorded the name change in his history, 'the place which has obtained the modern name of Bull-Ring, and which is used as a market for corn and herbs...'

Earlier in the same history, Hutton wrote that in the sixteenth century one John Cooper had obtained as one of three privileges from the Lord of the Manor: 'that he should, whenever he pleased, beat a bull in the Bull-ring [sic].' However, by the time of Hanson's survey bull-baiting had already been prohibited by Order in Council during 1773. It would continue to take place well outside the town though; eventually the barbaric pastime was stopped altogether in 1835 through an Act of Parliament.

Living conditions in many of the town's crowded streets and alleys improved with the passing of an Act of Parliament in 1769. This Act would see the creation of a body of men called the Street Commissioners, who had powers to clean the streets of Birmingham. They also widened the streets by demolishing houses, kept the streets safe, and lit them with oil lamps.

In 1765, Birmingham's first 'tourist attraction' was completed. From Matthew Boulton's Soho Manufactory small toys, buttons, buckles, boxes and japanned metal wares were being produced on a scale never seen before, with the pioneering of mass production using assembly line methods. Also, in 1773, thanks to Matthew Boulton's efforts, other Birmingham manufacturers would benefit from the establishment of the town's own assay office. Silverware would not have to be sent away to be stamped. Two years later, after he recognised the huge potential in James Watt's improvement of the Steam Engine, the famous partnership began that would power Britain's Industrial Revolution – literally.

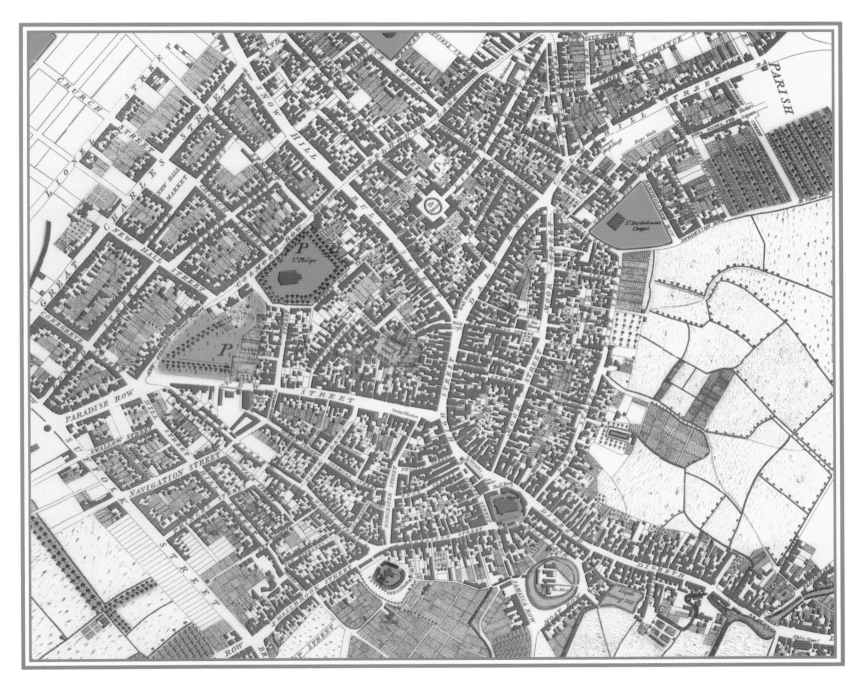

Plan of Birmingham, surveyed by Thomas Hanson, 1778. (Middle segment)

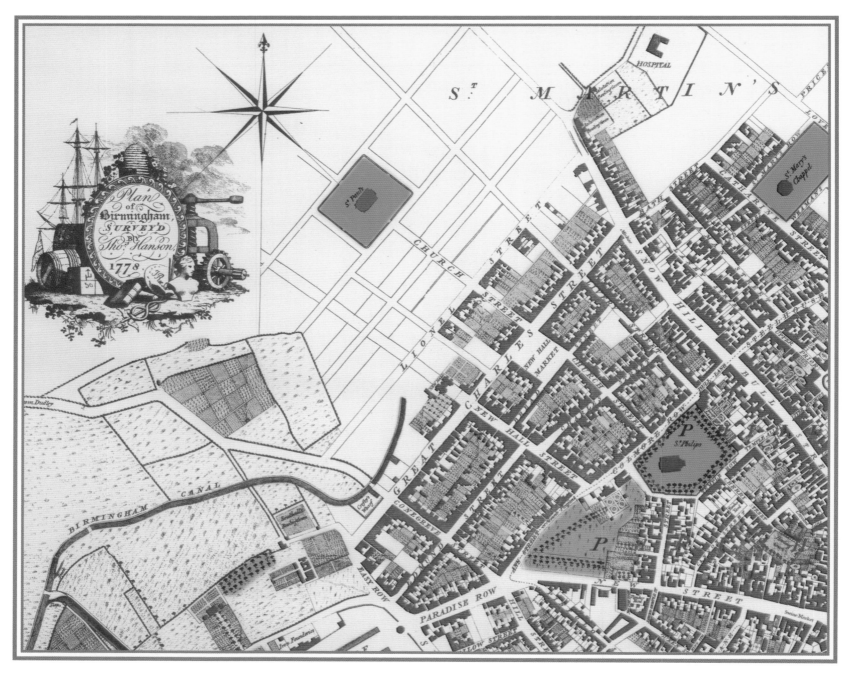

Plan of Birmingham, surveyed by Thomas Hanson, 1778. (Top left segment)

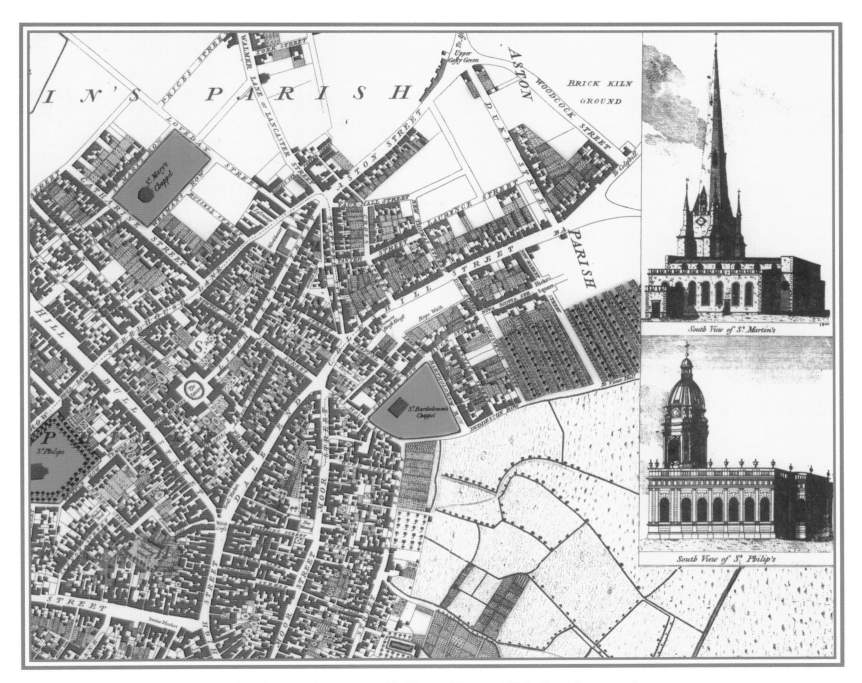

Plan of Birmingham, surveyed by Thomas Hanson, 1778. (Top right segment)

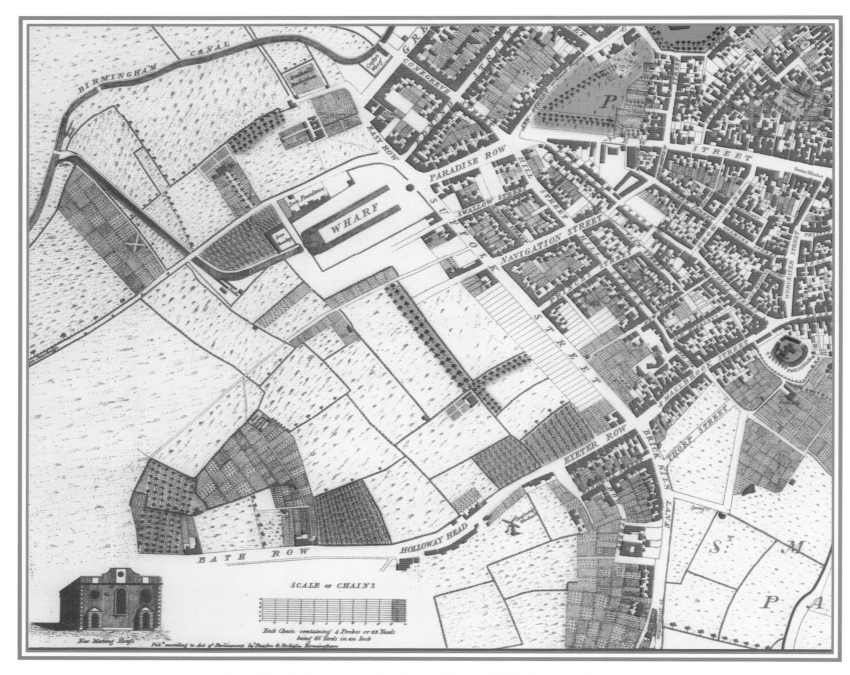

Plan of Birmingham, surveyed by Thomas Hanson, 1778. (Bottom left segment)

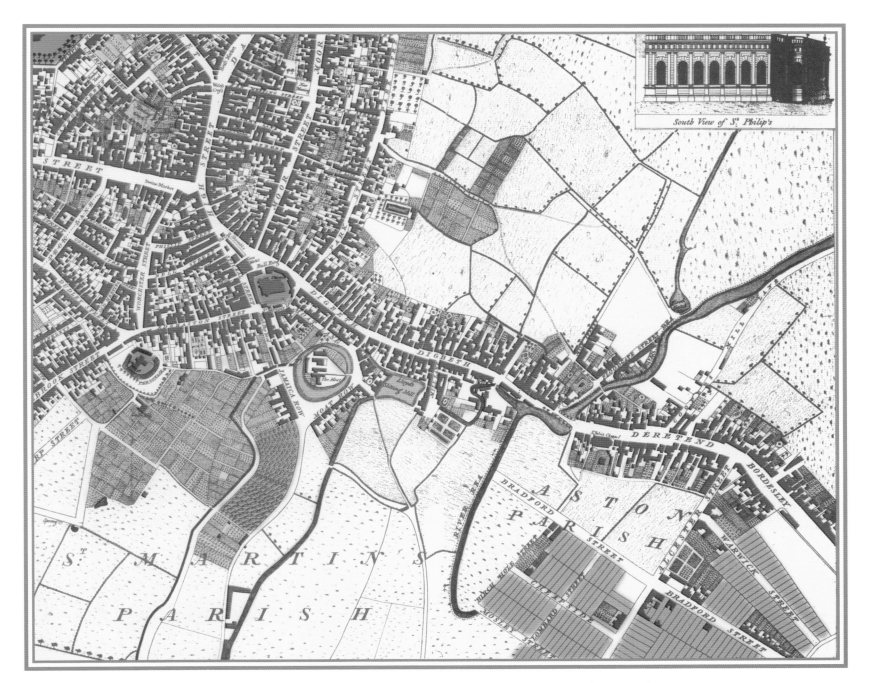

Plan of Birmingham, surveyed by Thomas Hanson, 1778. (Bottom right segment)

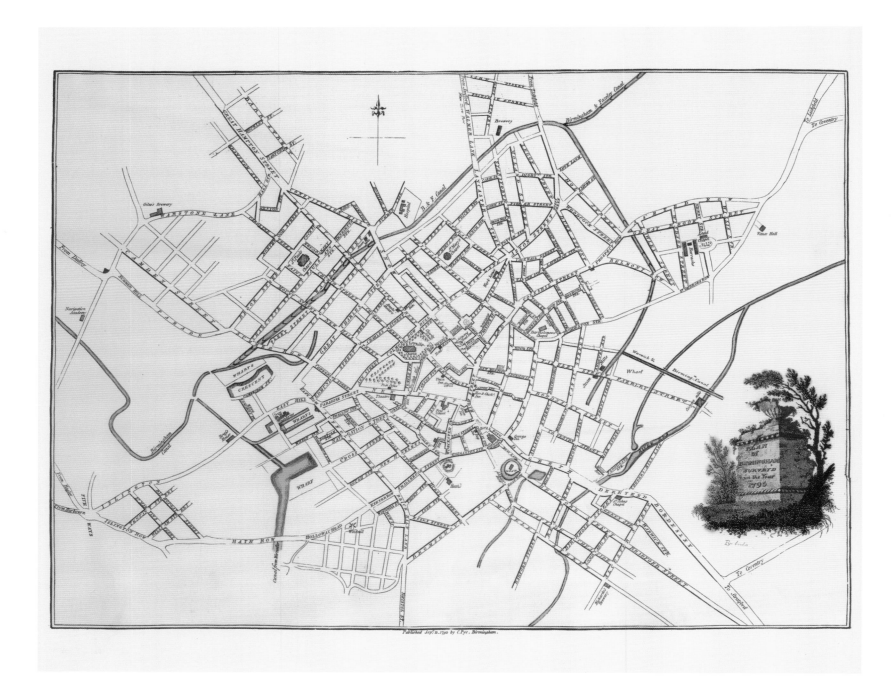

Plan of Birmingham, surveyed by Charles Pye, 1795.

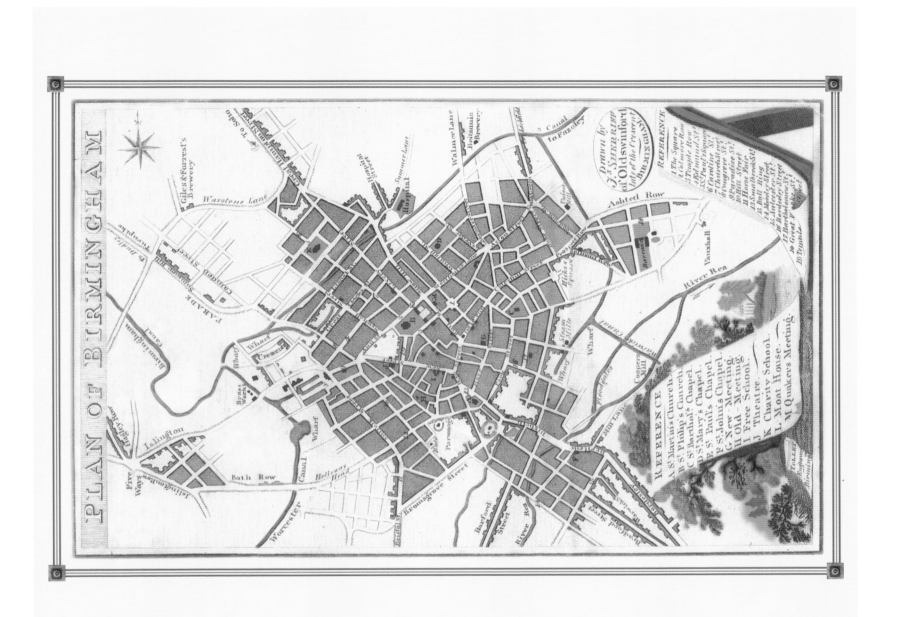

Plan of Birmingham, 1805, drawn by J.S. Sherriff and engraved by William Tolley.

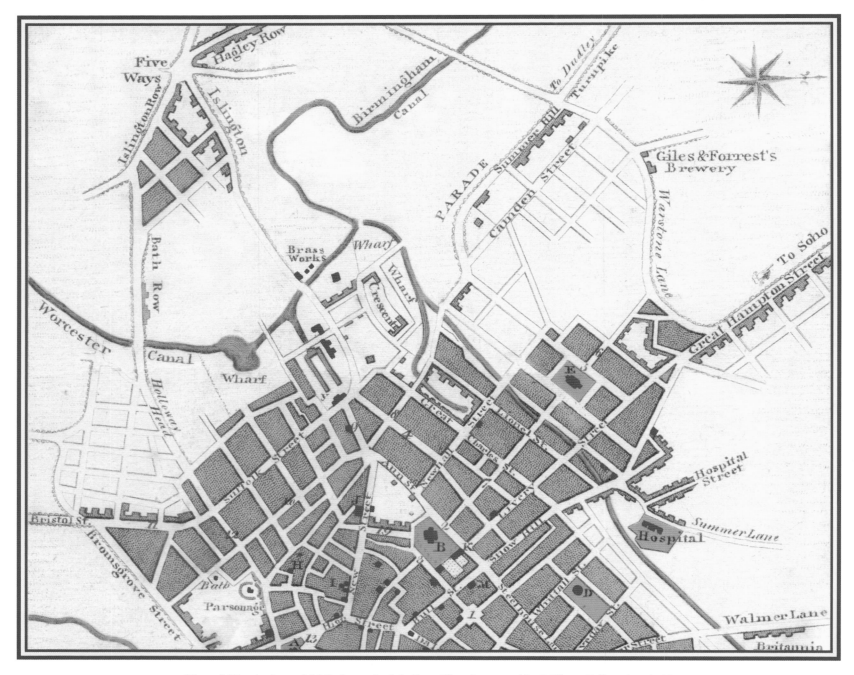

Plan of Birmingham, 1805, drawn by J.S. Sherriff and engraved by William Tolley. (Top half)

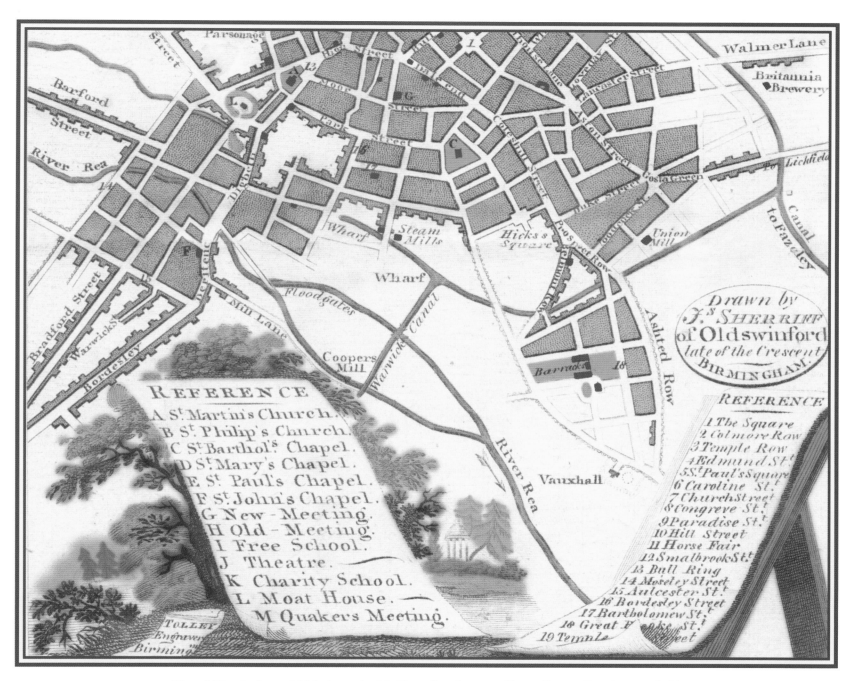

Plan of Birmingham, 1805, drawn by J.S. Sherriff and engraved by William Tolley. (Bottom half)

Six

FROM MOAT TO MARKET

Surveyor and land agent John Kempson's town plan of 1808 and his Borough Survey of 1810 show a number of changes in and around the further reaches of the borough. By comparing and studying the many maps, plans and surveys of Birmingham we can chart various events in the development of the town. However, we still have to rely on the accuracy of the information recorded at the time, and mistakes and

Old moated parsonage of St Martin's.

omissions did occur. In preparing the plans and surveys contained in the book we came across one such example.

John Kempson recorded that the water-filled moat around the parsonage of St Martin's, present on his 1808 town plan of Birmingham, had been filled in when producing his 1810 map of the town and borough of Birmingham. Later, when Wrightson published his book *Stranger's Guide to Birmingham* (written by Charles Pye), he included a town plan based on Kempson's 1808 town plan. He added relevant changes and new buildings to bring it up to date, but did not refer to the 1810 survey, therefore his 1819 plan still shows the moat around the parsonage. The plan by Josiah Robins, produced in 1816, substantiates this, showing only the moat around the old manor house. Robins' plan is delightful; he takes the trouble to show the area occupied by buildings in 1731 against the new area of Birmingham at the time of his plan in 1816.

Despite incorrectly showing the parsonage moat, Wrightson does record that the moat around the old manor house had been filled in and the remaining buildings demolished. The area where the old manor house

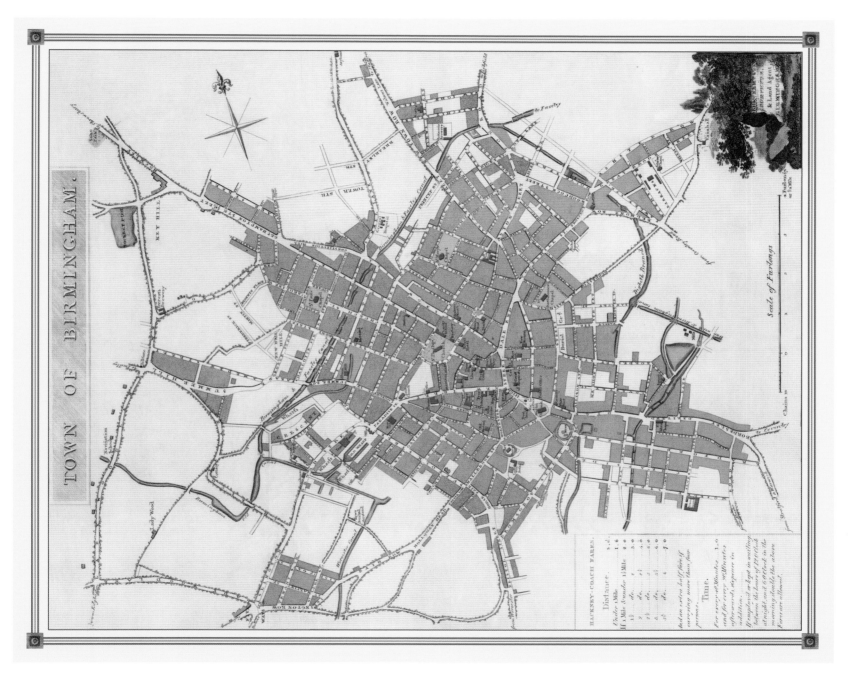

Plan of Birmingham, surveyed by John Kempson, 1808.

and moat stood became the site of the Smithfield Market, which was opened by the Street Commissioners on 29 May 1817. The parsonage itself was demolished in 1825.

Since Hanson's plan of 1778, a number of Birmingham's older buildings had disappeared. Around the market areas, the Old Cross was demolished in August 1784 and the Welsh Cross in March 1803. In the place where the Old Cross once stood, Birmingham's merchants were the first in Britain to commemorate a famous victory for England, erecting a statue of Admiral Nelson four years after his death at the Battle of Trafalgar in 1805. However, there were turbulent times ahead that would lead to the loss of buildings and the construction of new ones.

The barracks at Ashted (bottom right on Kempson's borough survey) were built in 1793; ensuring large military forces would be on hand in the event of trouble. Political and religious disputes were common in these times. The town of Birmingham already had a rich cultural mix of settlers from Europe and beyond; it also suffered from dissenters, in particular the Unitarians.

The catalyst for the permanent barracks came when Birmingham erupted in violence in 1791. They were called the Priestley Riots due to the fact that Joseph Priestley had upset the Church and some of the establishment with his radical ideas. By the time a large body of troops marched in from outside the town, extensive damage was done. Priestley's house at Fair Hill, Sparkbrook, was one of the first to be sacked and burned – his library and laboratory, with all his manuscripts, the record of life-long scientific and philosophical inquiries, perishing in the flames. The house and library of historian William Hutton were also destroyed. The Unitarian Meeting House, along with several houses belonging to members of the sect, was also burnt to the ground. As a result, Priestley left for America, never returning to Birmingham.

From the 1810 survey the built-up area is seen to be spreading in five directions: along the Bromsgrove and Wednesbury turnpikes, into Ashted and Highgate/Balsall Heath, between Newtown Road and Aston Road, and in the angle of the Worcester and Fazeley canals. There are two small detached developments: Summerhill/Camden Street, and the new suburb of Islington. The scattered hamlet of Winson Green and odd houses elsewhere are the only outliers.

Birmingham Heath was sold off by the manor as separate fields in 1798. Urbanisation began with a few high-class houses – built away from the smoke of the industrial town, but close enough for easy access via the Dudley and Wednesbury turnpikes.

Matthew Boulton's Soho Manufactory is also featured on the survey. However, with the passing of the great man himself in 1809, it would begin its steady decline. Back in 1788 he successfully established the Soho Mint alongside his manufactory, producing high-quality coins and medals. Since 1796, with the opening of the Soho Foundry (by the Birmingham canal, about a mile away), production of Boulton and Watts Steam Engines continued to be produced, powering a nation's industry.

Meeting House, destroyed by riots in 1791.

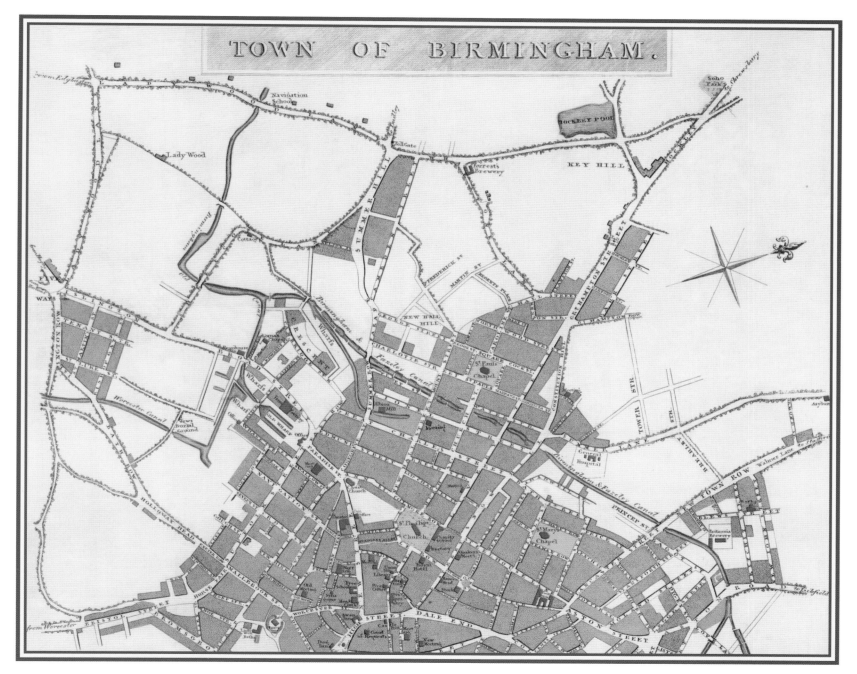

Plan of Birmingham, surveyed by John Kempson, 1808. (Top half)

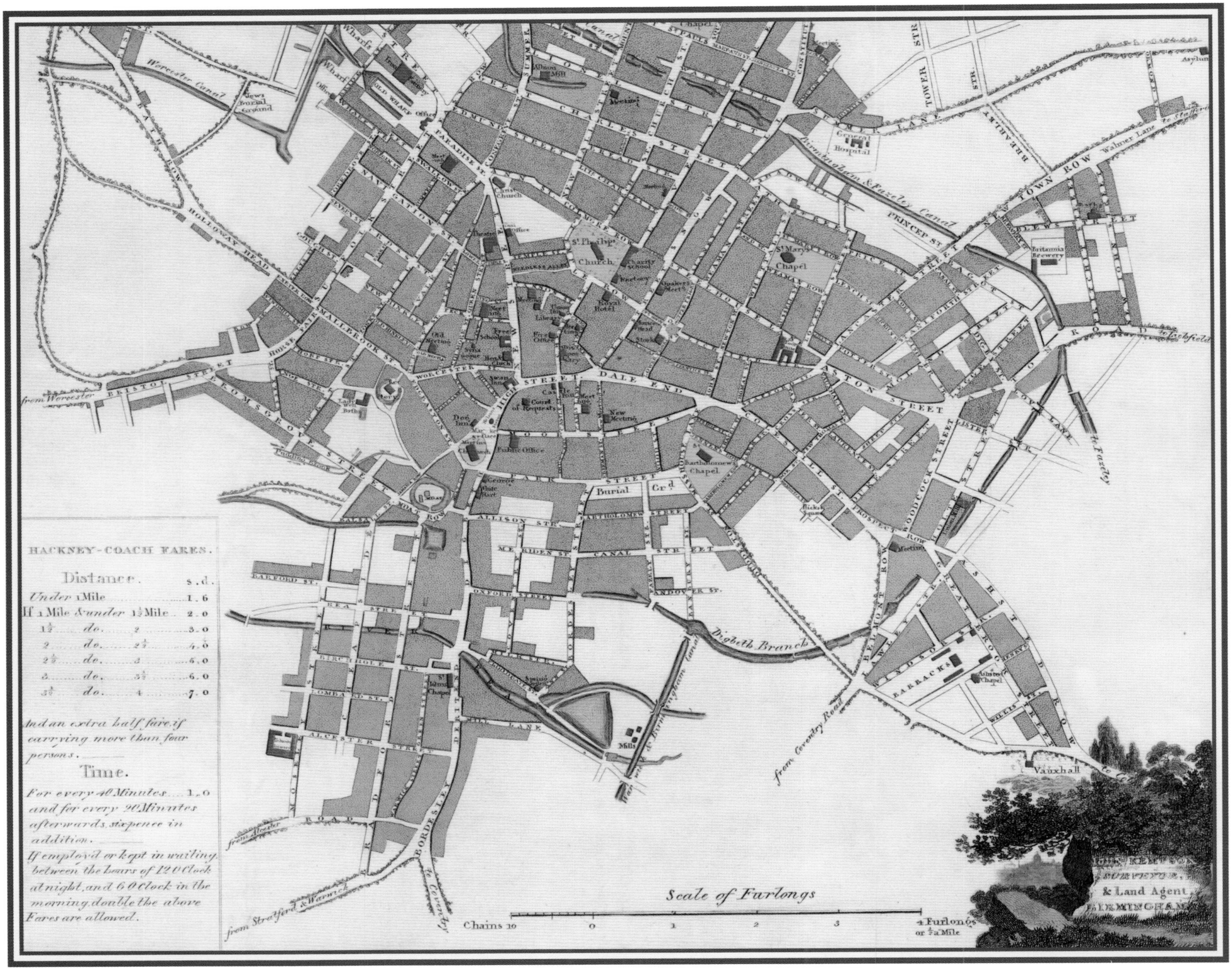

Plan of Birmingham, surveyed by John Kempson, 1808. (Bottom half)

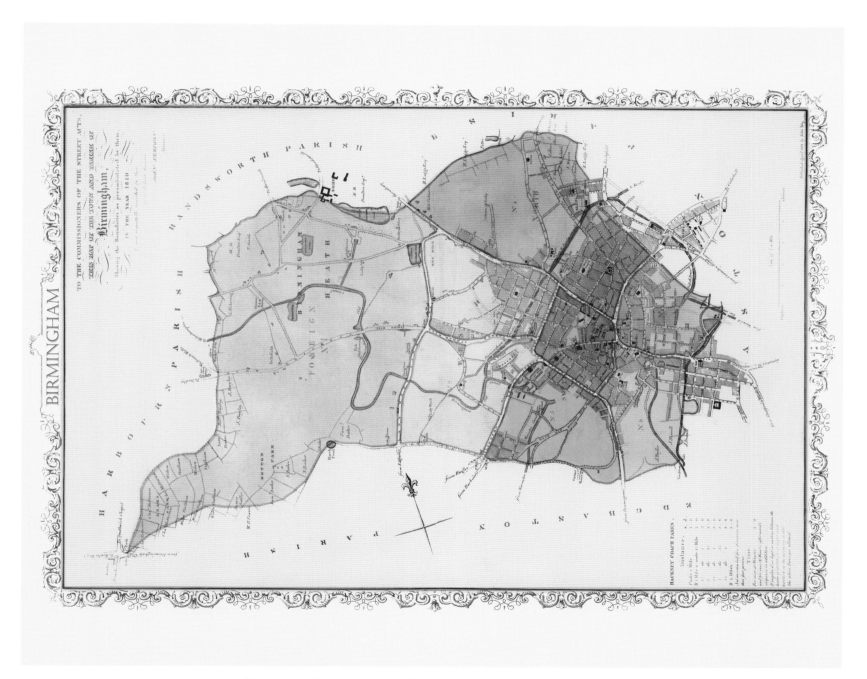

The town and parish of Birmingham, surveyed by John Kempson, 1810.

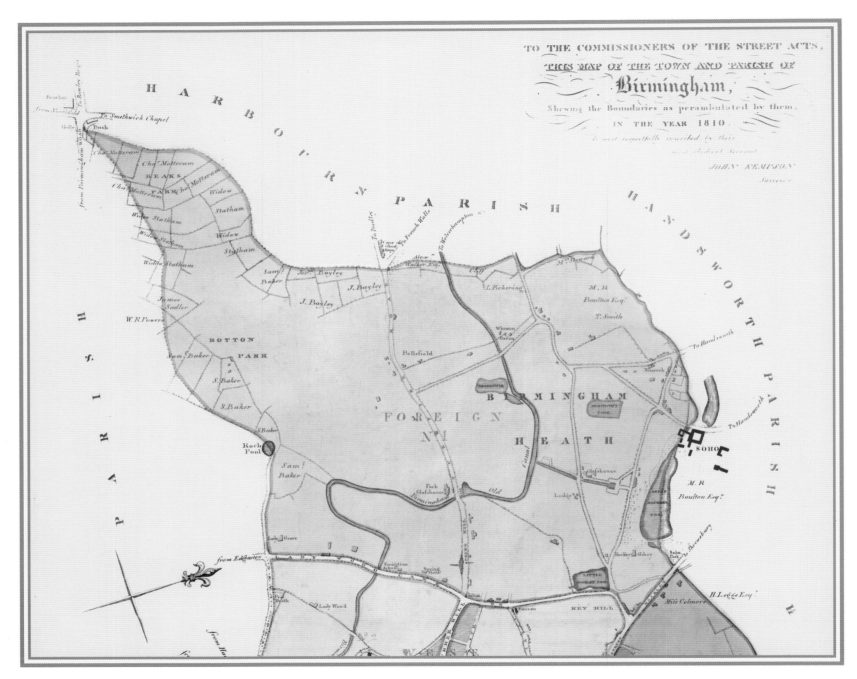

The town and parish of Birmingham, surveyed by John Kempson, 1810. (Top segment)

The town and parish of Birmingham, surveyed by John Kempson, 1810. (Middle segment)

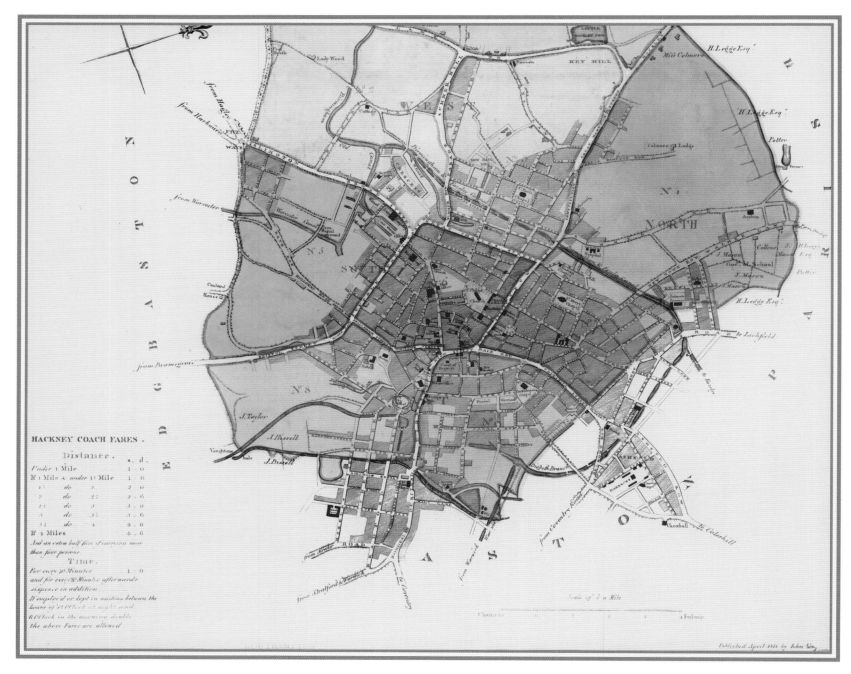

The town and parish of Birmingham, surveyed by John Kempson, 1810. (Bottom segment)

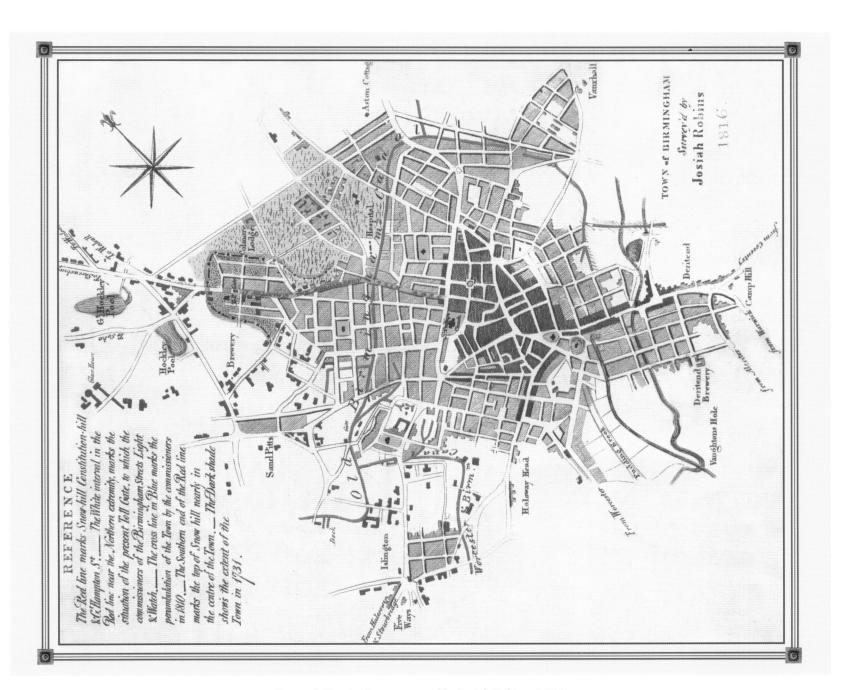

Town of Birmingham, surveyed by Josiah Robins, 1816.

Seven

QUEST FOR PARLIAMENTARY REFORM

Although the Priestley riots of 1791 caused unrest, violence and destruction, the events would be dwarfed against the national concern raised by the reform movement of the 1830s. Thomas Attwood, born not far from Birmingham in nearby Halesowen, would provide the

View down High Street, c. 1836.

leadership with which, through a series of vast public meetings, Birmingham would pave the way to securing Parliamentary Reform, which almost certainly saved the country from revolution.

Despite collecting 40,000 signatures on a petition calling for economic reform, Thomas Attwood failed to persuade the Duke of Wellington and his government to even consider his reformist ideas. Setbacks like this convinced Attwood that it was important that the basis of the House of Commons, which then represented only the landed interest, the Church, law and finance, should be broadened to include representatives from manufacturing towns like Birmingham, who knew a thing or two about business.

He therefore turned his mind to political reform and, in 1829, took the lead in establishing the Birmingham Political Union (BPU) to campaign for reform of the franchise and for representation for manufacturing towns. Other leaders were drawn not only from the town's elite but also from among its shopkeepers and small manufacturers. Supporters included a wide

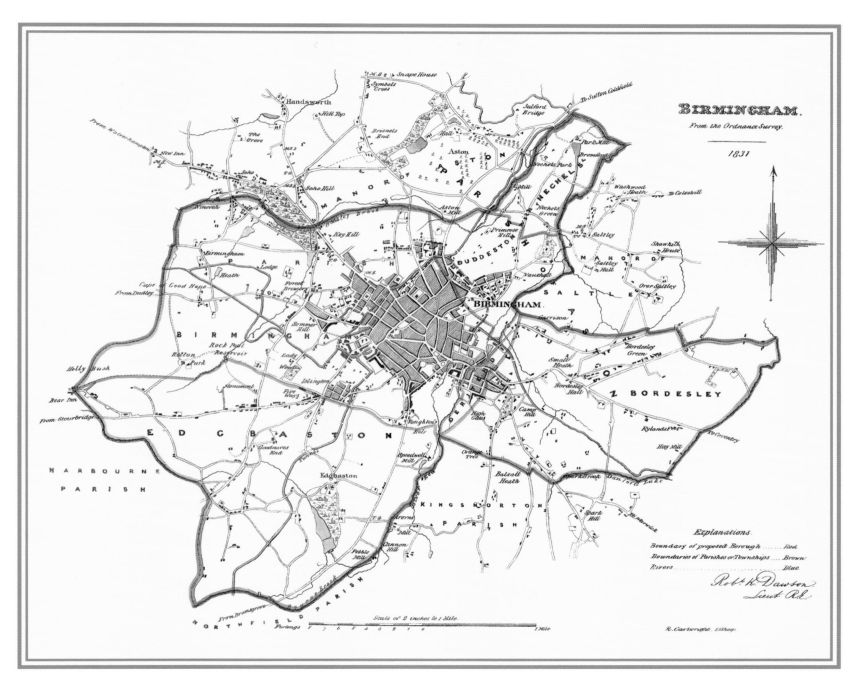

Birmingham, surveyed by Robert K. Dawson, 1831.

cross-section of the middle and working classes, and by the simple stratagem of holding vast public meetings that attracted the attention of the press, which reported the speeches to the nation, the BPU became the most effective agent in the campaign.

View of No. 101 High Street, Birmingham, c. 1836.

The Reform Act was passed on 4 June 1832. Attwood returned to Birmingham from London a hero. Massive crowds turned out to welcome him home. In the general election held in the autumn of that year, he and Joshua Scholefield, another leader of the BPU, became the first MPs for Birmingham.

Parliamentary constituencies were now reorganised, so new towns like Birmingham had their own MPs for the first time. Any man occupying, whether as a tenant or owner, houses of £10 a year value was given the vote. The value was taken either from the tax returns or parish rates, or from actual valuation where not let, or from the amount of rent. This greatly extended the number of men who had the right to vote.

As an integral part of this political change, Robert Dawson was commissioned to create detailed plans, produce surveys and report back to the government on any changes to city and borough boundaries throughout the land that might be considered necessary in order to complete the successful introduction of the Reform Act.

His plans, along with the Borough Survey of Birmingham 1831, showed the extent of the borough in question (in the form of the existing parish and borough boundaries) along with his proposals for expansion, as the survey team considered necessary. The plans were contained in three volumes, covering all counties along with reports. The survey report for Birmingham (*see* pages 63 and 64) is cause for nostalgia in its own right, and in it the survey team state that in their opinion, unoccupied land between the village of Soho and the town of Birmingham is unlikely to be built upon. Information is included regarding population, number of houses and taxes for Birmingham at the time.

Although Dawson's Birmingham plan only shows the built up town area in hatched lines, it gives ample detail further afield. From the distant village of Handsworth to Edgbaston in the south, by the end of the century these great tracts of land would be urbanised.

The plan presents a view of Thomas Telford's work; he was appointed chief engineer on 24 June 1824, soon after submitting his proposals. Telford ensured the much needed improvements to Birmingham's canal network were carried out. The 'straight line' cut is clearly shown improving the crucial transport link with the industries of the Black Country. As well as straightening and speeding up the canal journey, the canal was widened with tow paths for pulling horses on both sides.

Amid the squalor and open latrines of our industrial towns in the nineteenth century lurked death. Typhoid, typhus, smallpox, cholera, rickets, scarlet fever, measles, whooping cough, diphtheria, and diarrhoea thrived. The first cholera outbreak of 1831-32 passed from Manchester to the nearby small manufacturing towns of the Black Country. The effects were little short of catastrophic. In one of these towns, Bilston, there were 3,568 cases and 693 deaths; in other local towns in this manufacturing district the number of deaths varied from fifty to over 200. It is of interest that Birmingham, the largest industrial town nearby, suffered only twenty-one deaths. As with the plague back in the seventeenth century, Birmingham had escaped lightly, however the state of public health in the town would soon get far worse. Without a clean supply of piped water, only that from wells, and no method of dealing with raw sewage, many Birmingham people succumbed to deadly diseases.

BIRMINGHAM.

REPORT on the TOWN of BIRMINGHAM.

THE Limits described in the second Column of Schedule (C) of the late Bill comprise the whole of what can with propriety be called the Town of *Birmingham*. The only point at which the line of Boundary runs near to any considerable mass of buildings which is not within it, is where the Boundary of the Parish of Birmingham runs along Hockley Brook. On the North of this Brook is the Village of Soho, in the Parish of Handsworth. It is, however, separated from the Town by a considerable interval of unoccupied ground, which is low, and not likely to be built upon. The Brook is also the Boundary of the two Counties, and forms so obvious a separation, that were it overstept for the sake of including Soho, there seems no reason why the limit should not be indefinitely stretched, so as to include a number and succession of populous Villages occurring at intervals upon the roads towards Dudley and Wolverhampton.

We recommend that the Contents of the future Borough should be as follows:

THE Parish of Birmingham, the Parish of Edgbaston, and the Townships of Bordesley, Duddeston and Nechels, and Deritend. *Proposed Contents of the Borough.*

I. J. Chapman

W. H. Ord.

TABLE exhibiting the Condition of the PARISH of BIRMINGHAM and of the proposed Borough.

BIRMINGHAM.	Population, 1821.	Population, 1831.	Houses, 1821.	Houses, 1831.	Houses worth £.10. a year and upwards.	Assessed Taxes.
Parish of Birmingham	85,416	110,914	18,571	24,339	5,470	£. s. d. —
Within the proposed Limits - - -	106,722	142,251	—	30,000	7,000	28,350 18 9¼

Reform Act survey report for Birmingham.

SUMMARY of all the INFORMATION relative to *Birmingham*, laid before Parliament since March 1831.

1.—*Limits proposed:*

Rep.

Comprise the Parish of Birmingham, the Parish of Edgbaston, and the Townships of Bordesley, Deritend, and Duddeston with Nechels.

2.—*Population:*

	In 1821.	In 1831.
Parl. Ret. 418. 334. Of the proposed Borough - - - - -	106,722	142,251

3.—*Number of Houses:* *

	1828.	Worth £. 10 a year, and upwards.
Parl. Ret. 314, 5. In the Parishes of Saint Mary and Saint Philip, Birmingham - - - - - } †	21,971	4,902
Ditto. In the Parish of Edgbaston - - - -	,,	533
Ditto. In Deritend District - - - - -	,,	617
Ditto. In Duddeston and Nechels District - - -	,,	480
In the proposed Borough (omitting Bordesley) - -	,,	6,532

4.—*Amount of Assessed Taxes paid:*

	1828.			1829.			1830.		
	£.	s.	d.	£.	s.	d.	£.	s.	d.
By the Town within the proposed Boundary - }	26,929	18	5	27,804	1	9¼	28,350	18	9¼

5.—*Number of Persons rated to the relief of the Poor:*

	Persons paying
Parl. Ret. 316. Within the Parishes of Saint Martin and Saint Philip † - - -	4,450

---

* These Returns refer to January 1828.

† The whole of the Parish of Birmingham, which is divided for Ecclesiastical purposes only.

Reform Act survey report for Birmingham, 1832.

View of Birmingham from Bordesley Fields, 1836.

Eight

DAWNING OF THE RAILWAY AGE

Drawn and engraved by John Dower FRGS of Pentonville, London, in 1834, this detailed plan shows Birmingham's development continuing apace on the edges of the town. Likewise, right in the heart of the town, one of the last pieces of land that made up the triangle between New Street, Anne Street (now Colmore Row) and Temple Street had now been built upon, with the cutting of Waterloo Street and Bennett's Hill made between 1825 and 1827.

View of Bennett's Hill, 1814 – the seat of William Hutton Esq.

By now there were many factories, but, unlike the cotton towns of the north-west, the town was heavily dependent upon workshops. Despite having the most important steam engine production facility in the land, Boulton and Watt's steam engines were not widely used in Birmingham. Thousands of workshops were occupied by small numbers of workers who used hand rather than steam power to operate presses, stamps and early lathes.

Not long after Matthew Boulton had passed away, his business partner, James Watt, retired. Production passed to the control of their sons, Matthew Robinson Boulton and James Watt Junior. Using the latest manufacturing and assembly techniques, they ensured continued production of their steam engines well after their own passing, right up to 1895.

The development of large industrial premises along the canals encircling the town centre had a profound effect. It ceased to be a pleasant place to live. Many of the prosperous middle classes with wealth at their disposal moved out to the leafy new suburbs, building many magnificent mansions, exemplifying their new-found wealth. One such

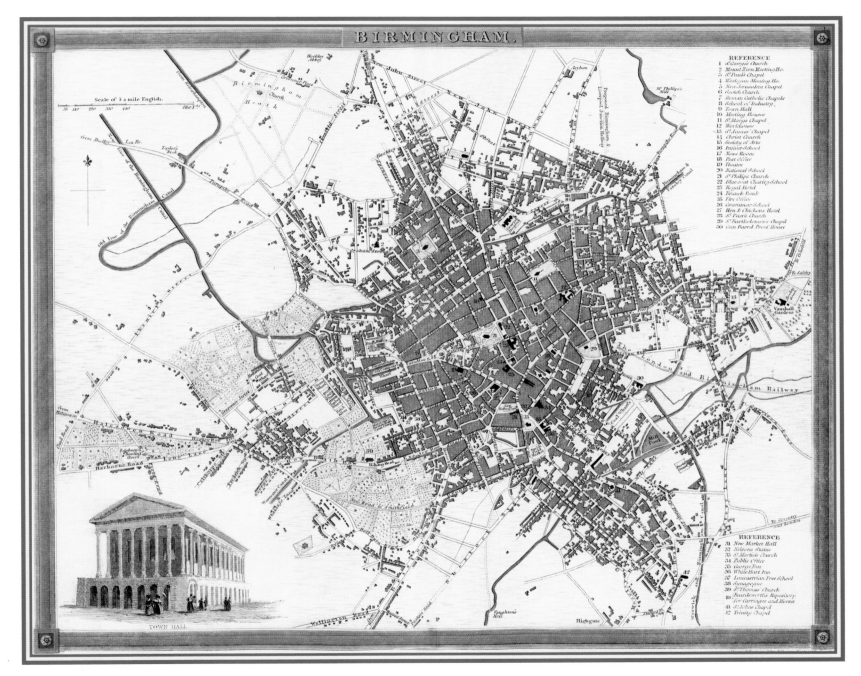

Birmingham, 1834, drawn and engraved by John Dower.

Georgian mansion to the north of the town, on Lozells Lane, was significant enough to have the district named after it, many years before the historic football club that adopted that name was conceived – Aston Villa. Back in the heart of the town, that once premier address, the Old Square, was to become a slum.

The view across Birmingham from the early 1830s, featured on page 74, shows the contrast between the almost rural aspects in the foreground, to the skyline of Birmingham, with its belching factory chimneys already dominating the skyline. However, the view (reference the view from the same spot featured on page 89) would change significantly within the same decade – as with many expanses of land and water courses across the country, the railway age had already dawned.

The Bill for the Grand Junction Railway, which was named after the Newton-le-Willows junction, was passed in Parliament on 6 May 1833. This was the same day on which the Bill for the London and Birmingham Railway was passed. Work on both lines was now proceeding at a fast pace.

John Dower, like many surveyors before him, and those that would follow, strove to ensure that his work was as up-to-date as possible. He took the initiative in marking the planned entry routes of the first major trunk railways to be constructed. Unfortunately, he could not have predicted that the actual route into Birmingham for the Grand Junction Railway from Liverpool would be considerably different from the original agreed route.

The London line was to terminate in Birmingham at an impressive station to be built in Curzon Street. It seems that the original plan was for a Grand Junction Railway terminus off Pritchett Street, Aston, presumably with an end on link with the London line at Curzon Street. Not every plan runs smoothly; James Watt Junior, who had acquired the tenancy of Aston Hall in 1831, was not on his own in objecting to intrusion so close to his house. He insisted the railway should run to the north of Aston parish church, looping through Duddeston to a station near to Curzon Street, with a connection for through trains. There were also engineering difficulties that had not been fully considered when planning the direct approach into Birmingham. The solution, requiring a further Act of Parliament, would lead to its long curving revised approach into Birmingham, coming in from the east alongside the London and Birmingham line.

The Town Hall, illustrated on the plan, opened on 19 September 1834. Its design was based on the Parthenon in Greece, by the architect Joseph Hansom, who also designed the Hansom Cab. Although opened in 1834, it was not finished until 1849 and the later stages of its construction were carried out by another architect, Charles Edge. Upon its opening, visitors to Birmingham's Town Hall were awestruck not only by the building's impressive Roman Revival civic architecture, but also by the magnificence of the specially commissioned organ. Like the hall itself, the organ had been built and designed first and foremost to meet the needs and demands of the Birmingham Triennial Music Festivals.

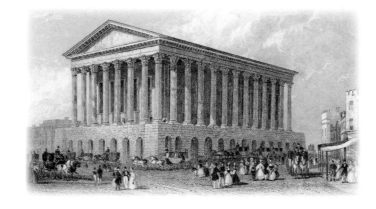

Birmingham Music Festival was held on 7, 8, 9 & 10 October 1834 at the Town Hall.

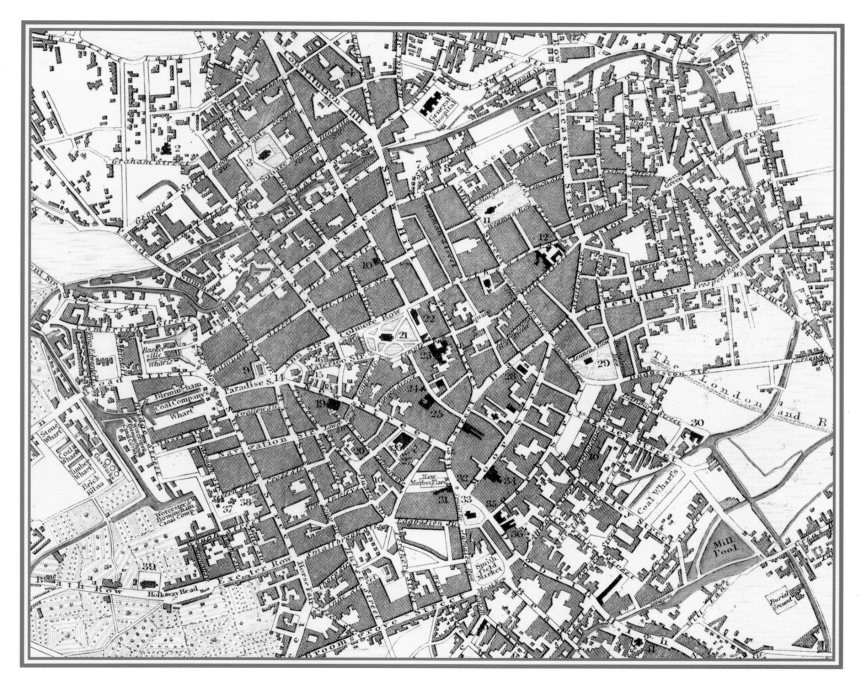

Birmingham, 1834, drawn and engraved by John Dower. (Middle segment)

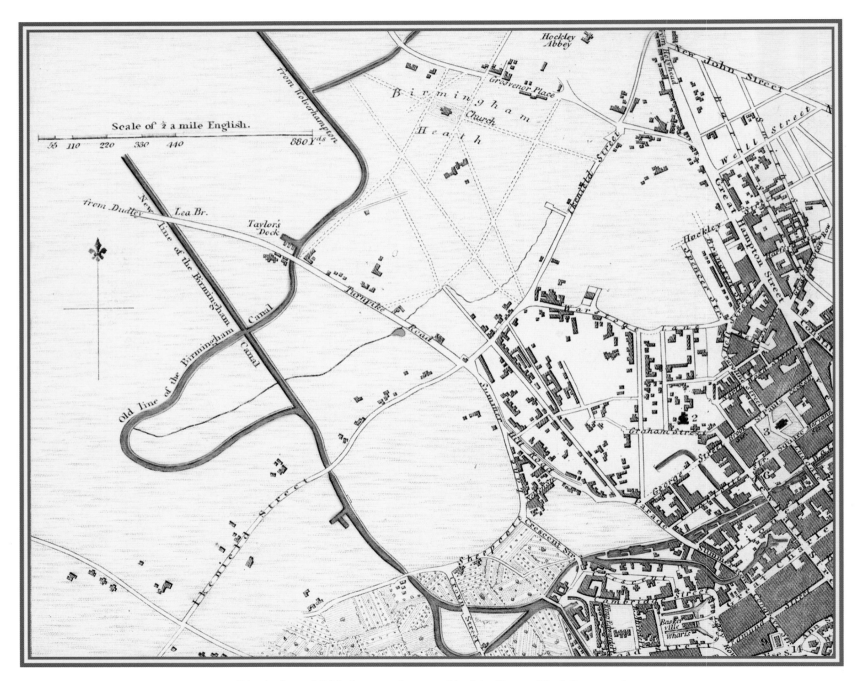

Birmingham, 1834, drawn and engraved by John Dower. (Top left segment)

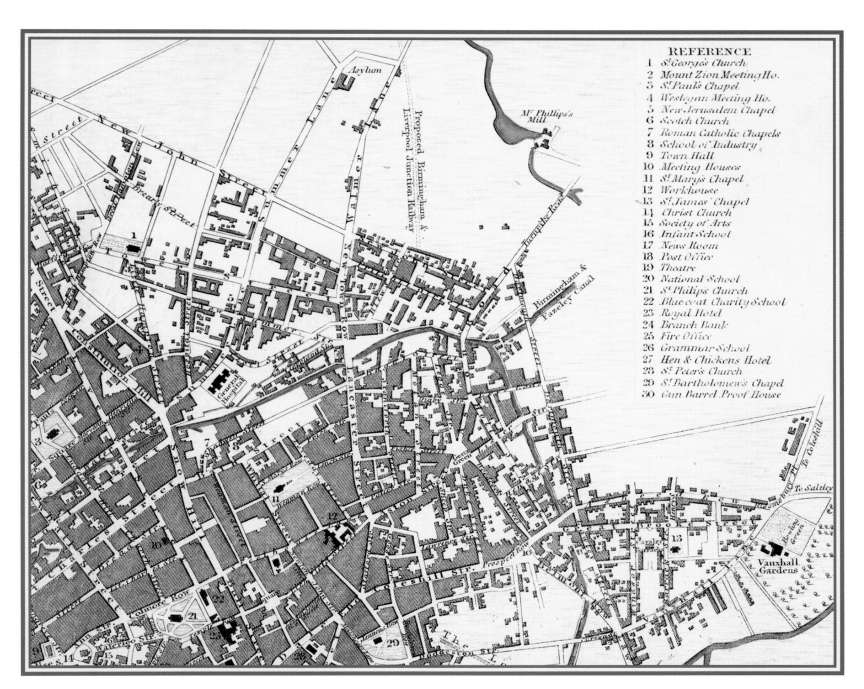

REFERENCE

1 St George's Church
2 Mount Zion Meeting Ho.
3 St Paul's Chapel
4 Wesleyan Meeting Ho.
5 New Jerusalem Chapel
6 Scotch Church
7 Roman Catholic Chapels
8 School of Industry
9 Town Hall
10 Meeting Houses
11 St Mary's Chapel
12 Workhouse
13 St James' Chapel
14 Christ Church
15 Society of Arts
16 Infant School
17 News Room
18 Post Office
19 Theatre
20 National School
21 St Philips Church
22 Blue coat Charity School
23 Royal Hotel
24 Branch Bank
25 Fire Office
26 Grammar School
27 Hen & Chickens Hotel
28 St Peter's Church
29 St Bartholomew's Chapel
30 Gun Barrel Proof House

Birmingham, 1834, drawn and engraved by John Dower. (Top right segment)

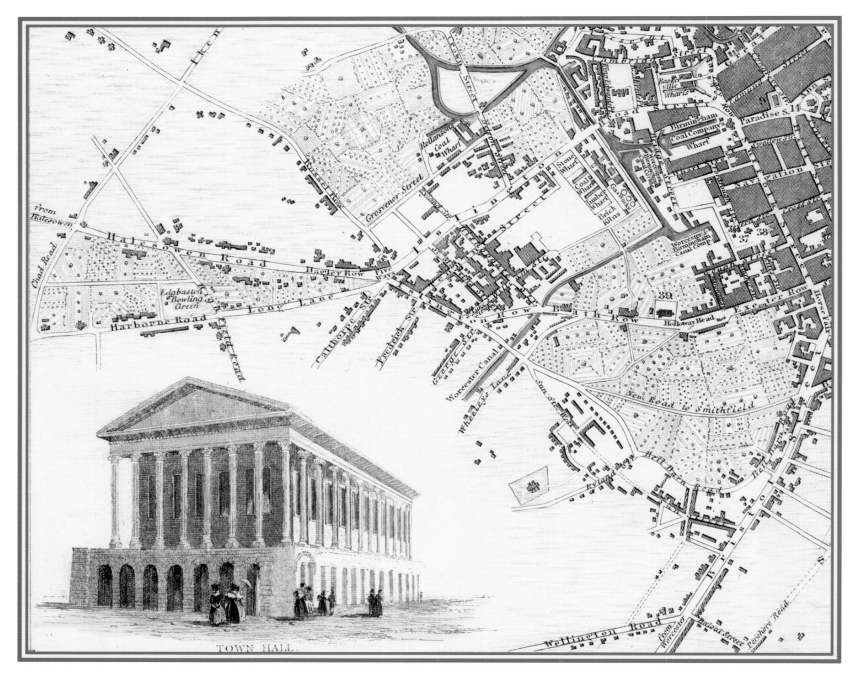

Birmingham, 1834, drawn and engraved by John Dower. (Bottom left segment)

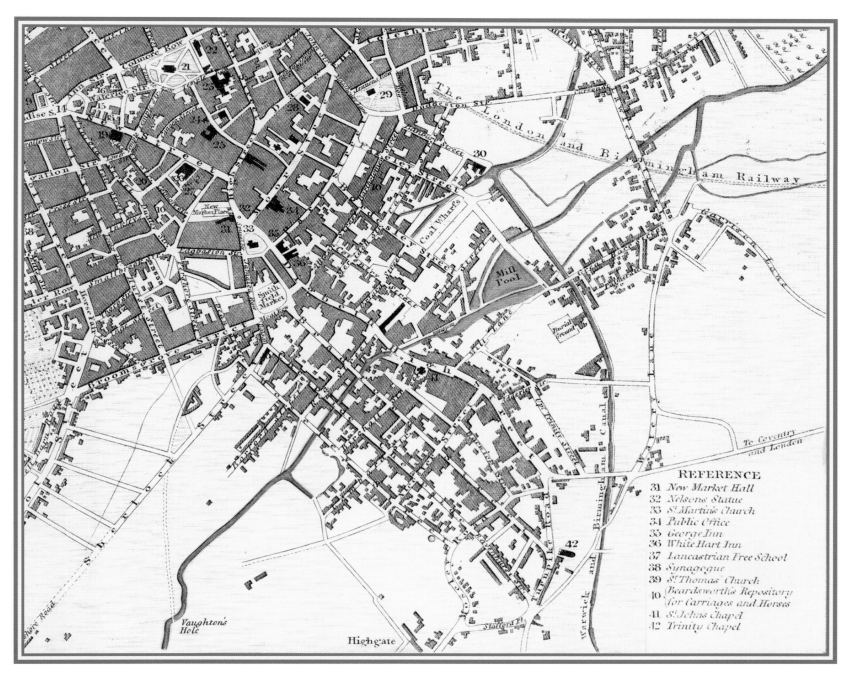

Birmingham, 1834, drawn and engraved by John Dower. (Bottom right segment)

REFERENCE
31 New Market Hall
32 Nelsons Statue
33 St Martin's Church
34 Public Office
35 George Inn
36 White Hart Inn
37 Lancastrian Free School
38 Synagogue
39 St Thomas' Church
40 Beardsworth's Repository for Carriages and Horses
41 St Johns Chapel
42 Trinity Chapel

View of Birmingham prior to the coming of the railway, c. 1830.

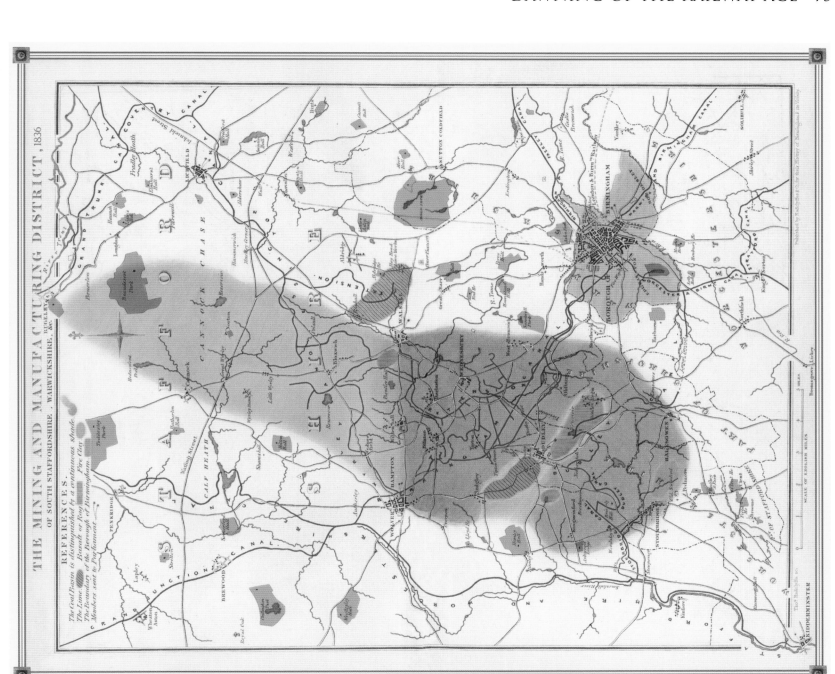

Map showing the Black Country and Birmingham, published 1836.

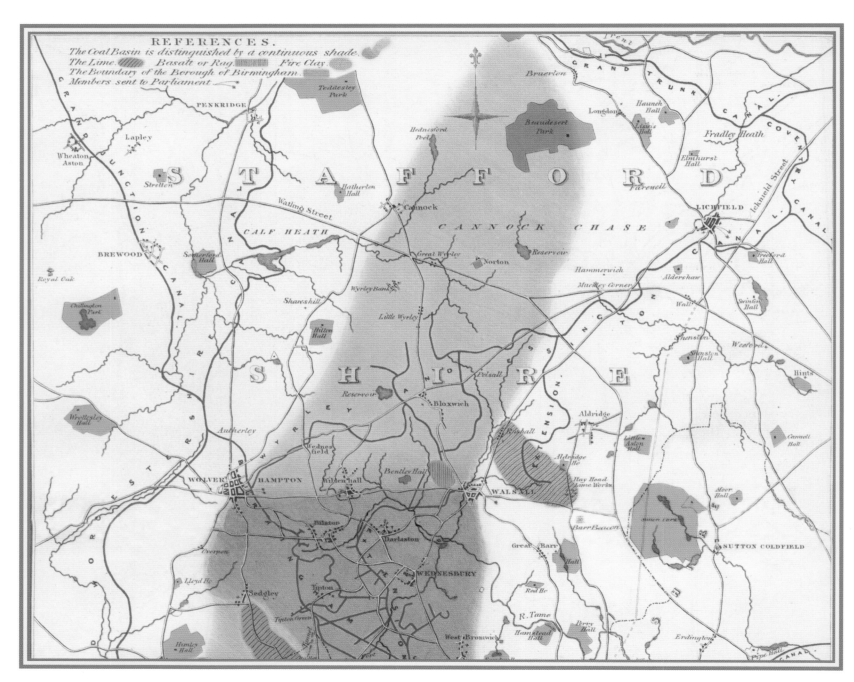

Map showing the Black Country and Birmingham, published 1836. (Top half)

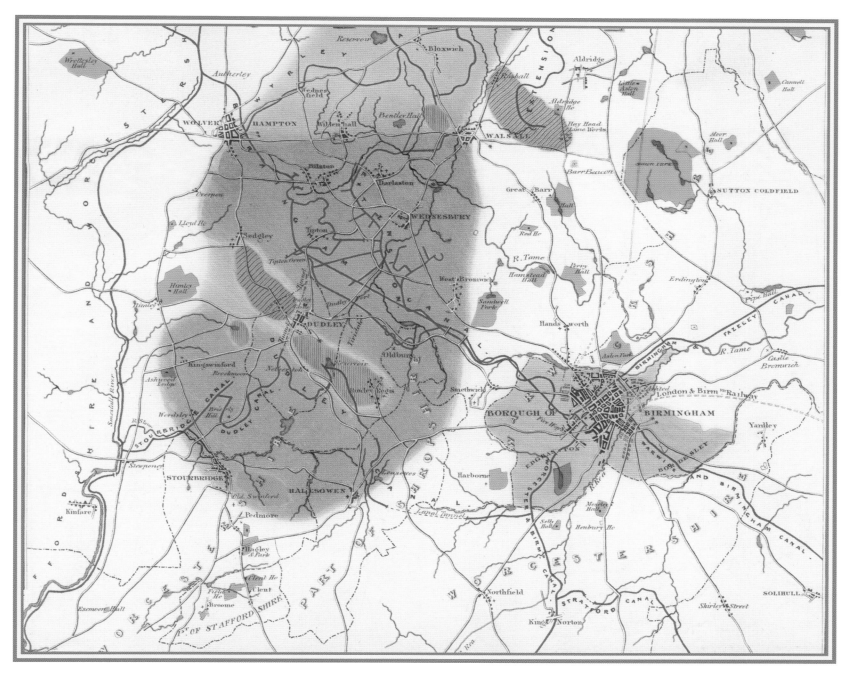

Map showing the Black Country and Birmingham, published 1836. (Bottom half)

Nine
ARRIVAL OF THE IRON HORSE

Benevolent societies whose intentions were to disseminate knowledge were a distinguishing feature of the Victorian age. The Society for the Diffusion of Useful Knowledge (SDUK) was founded in 1827 by John Earl Russell and Henry Brougham, later Chancellor of England. Earl Russell, an MP, was responsible for setting up an inspectorate for schools and for supplying an additional grant of £30,000 for education.

Curzon Street Station.

The society published books and atlases that were deemed to be of high educational worth, but produced them at a price that was affordable. Their greatest publication was their atlas of the world, entitled 'Maps of the Society for the Diffusion of Useful Knowledge'. The fine steel engravings are hand-coloured and are often embellished with vignettes and comparisons of the height of the principal buildings of the town or city, as with the Birmingham plan of 1839.

As the eighteenth century had been the period of canal construction, the nineteenth was to be the century of railway making. Birmingham men were shrewd enough to hail the coming of the 'iron horse', and gave hearty support to the new movement.

Despite the late change to the route of the Grand Junction Railway (that had required the hasty design and construction of several extra bridges, viaducts and embankments as well as diverting the course of the river Tame), it was completed in record time and within budget. It was also a great personal triumph for the railway engineer now in charge, Joseph Locke.

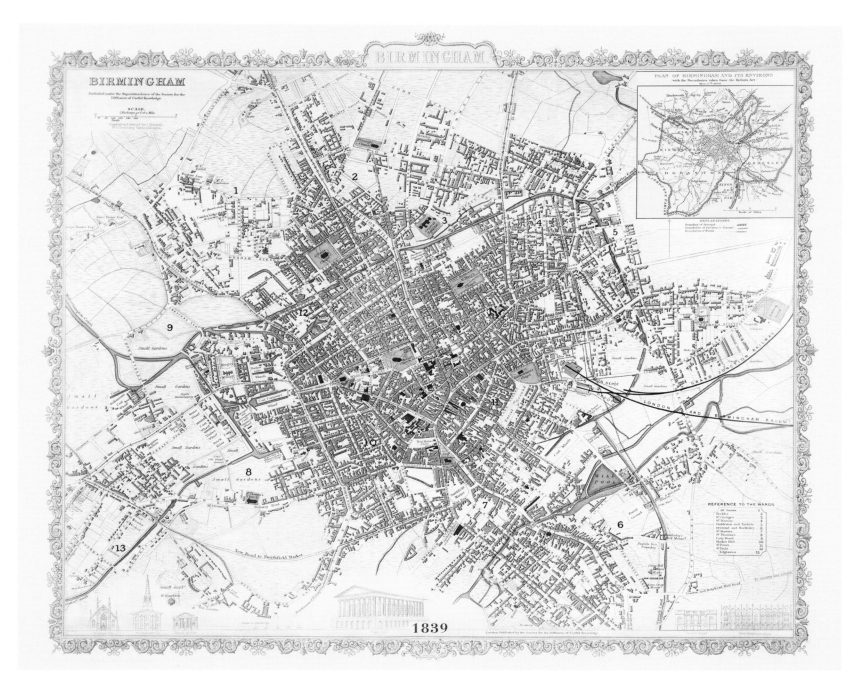

Plan of Birmingham, 1839, from the Society for the Diffusion of Useful Knowledge (SDUK).

The Grand Junction Railway company opened a temporary terminus at Vauxhall and the first train arrived from Liverpool in July 1837.

The following year saw the London and Birmingham railway complete their line from London Euston, terminating at their new station at Curzon Street. The station was built on the edge of the town, without a decent road connection. This caused increasing problems as the railway system expanded, yet it would be well over twenty years before trains would reach the heart of the town.

The first London to Birmingham train arrived at Curzon Street on Monday 17 September 1838. A year later, in 1839, the Grand Junction Railway extended their line from Vauxhall into Curzon Street, setting up their terminus adjacent to their rival, the London and Birmingham Railway.

Such was the competition to establish transport links with the city of Birmingham that in 1839 the third company to arrive was the Birmingham and Derby Railway. This was followed by a fourth company in 1841, the Birmingham and Gloucester railway.

The importance of the railways and the subsequent impact on Birmingham commerce cannot be over-estimated. Manufactured goods could now move at a speed and efficiency that would have been unimaginable just a few years previously. Long distance journeys that once took weeks could now be done in a day. Although this issued the death

The old Market Hall.

warrant of the canals, which would deteriorate rapidly over the coming years, the manufacturing powerhouse of the world would benefit immensely as a result.

The SDUK Plan of Birmingham shows the division of council wards. The first wards, a total of thirteen, are numbered on the plan and table. Birmingham's charter of incorporation was received in 1838, following the passing of the Municipal Corporation Act in 1835. It was read in the Town Hall on 5 November with elections for the first town council held on 26 December. Sixteen aldermen and forty-eight councillors were elected. William Scholefield became the first mayor and William Redfern was appointed town clerk.

The plan shows the re-built King Edward VI Grammar School, on the corner of Peck Lane and New Street. Charles Barry had won the competition to re-build the school on its original site in 1832. The resulting masterpiece was opened in 1838, a monument to Victorian gothic architecture with exemplary interior design by the celebrated Pugin. Unfortunately, due to development in the area, the building would only remain for 100 years.

Following the need for a sheltered market hall in the Bull Ring area, Birmingham's grand Market Hall was completed in 1835. The Market Hall was elegantly designed by the same architect who completed the later stages of the Town Hall. It contained 600 market stalls with a front façade made from the stone mined in Bath, Somerset. Impressive Doric columns supported the entrances, closed at night with large metal gates.

Over a hundred years later, the Luftwaffe almost ended its busy days. The building was gutted by the incendiary bomb, but despite being roofless the hall was still in use until it was bulldozed as part of the 1960s development of the Bull Ring.

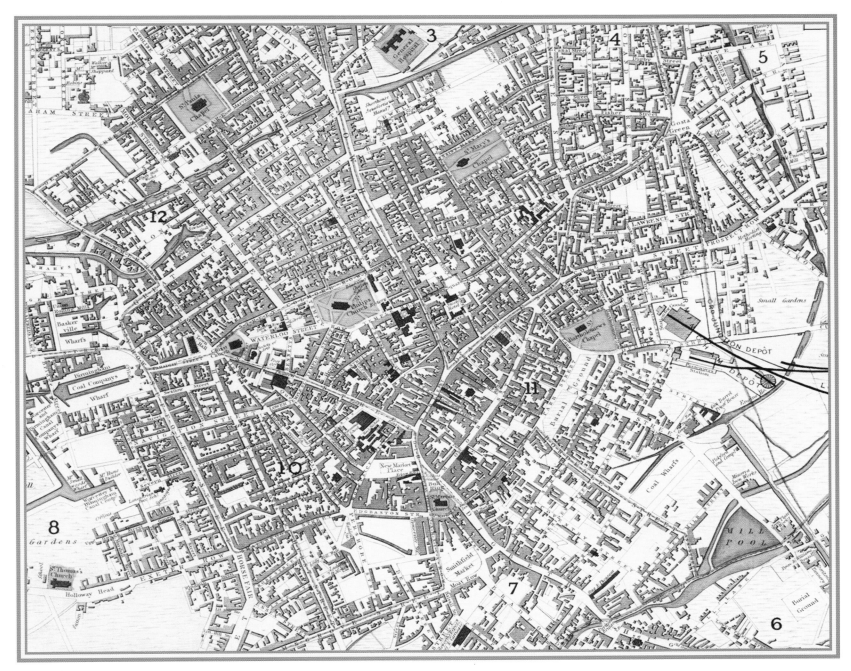

Plan of Birmingham, 1839, from the Society for the Diffusion of Useful Knowledge (SDUK). (Middle segment)

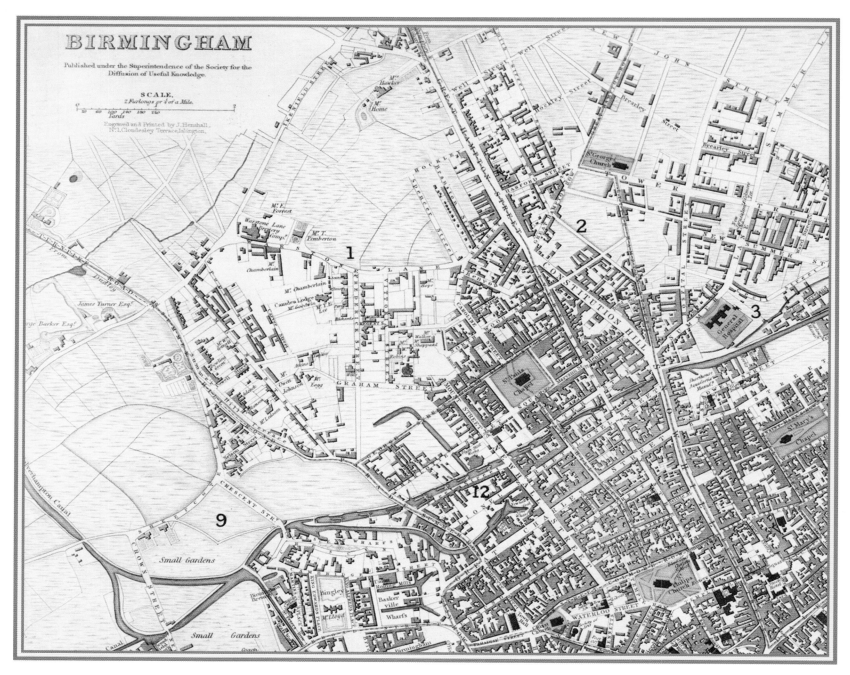

Plan of Birmingham, 1839, from the Society for the Diffusion of Useful Knowledge (SDUK). (Top right segment)

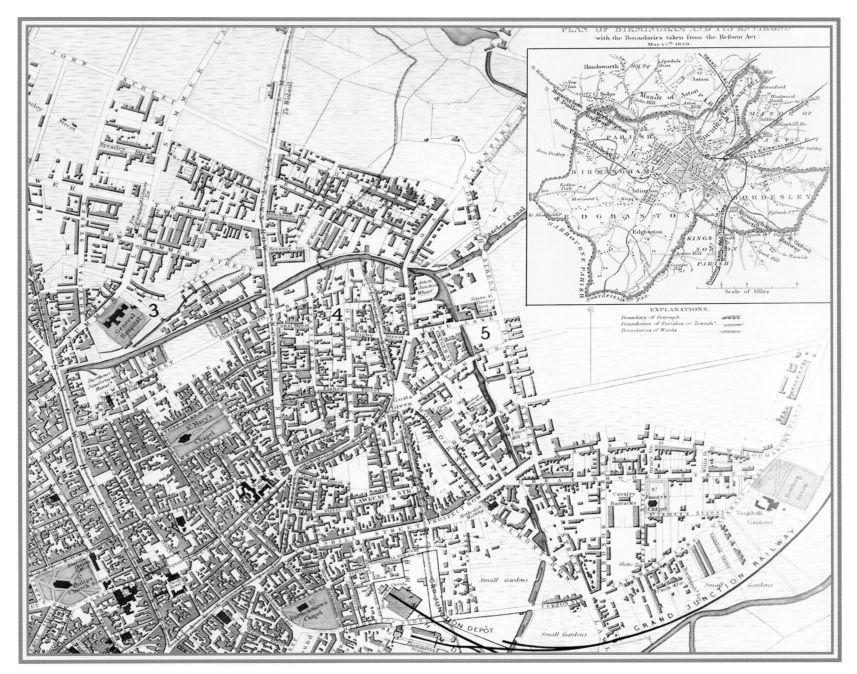

Plan of Birmingham, 1839, from the Society for the Diffusion of Useful Knowledge (SDUK). (Top right segment)

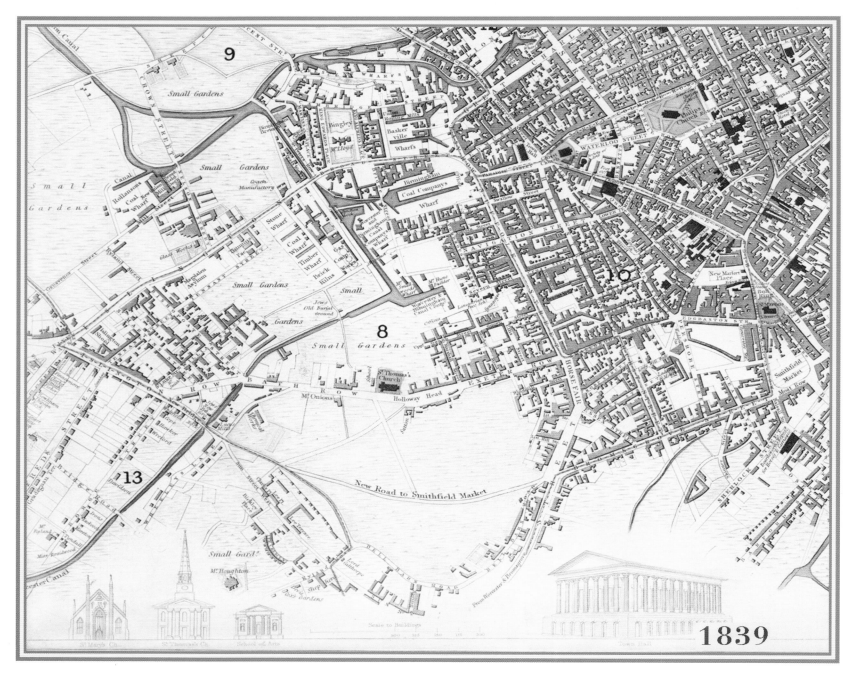

Plan of Birmingham, 1839, from the Society for the Diffusion of Useful Knowledge (SDUK). (Bottom left segment)

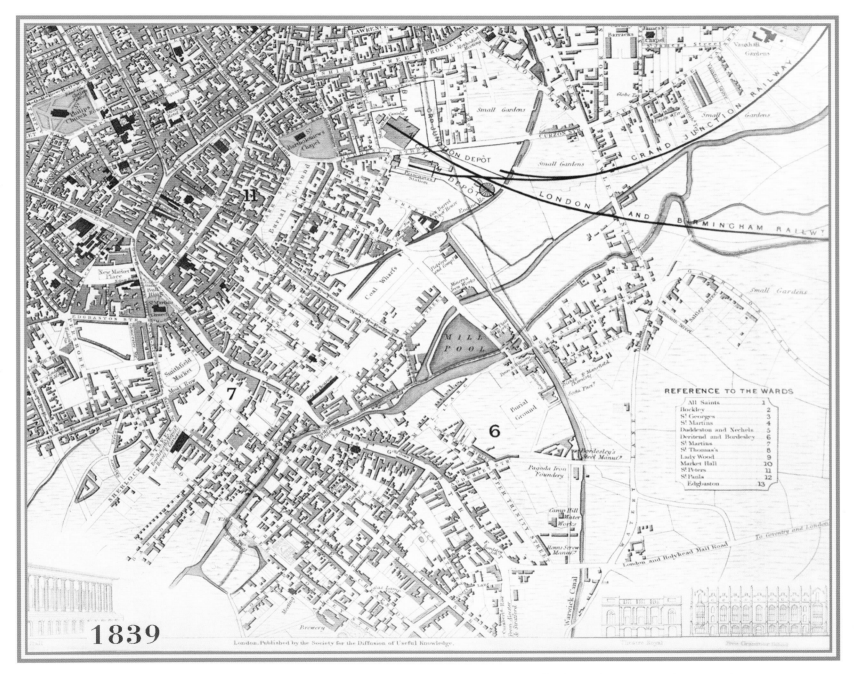

Plan of Birmingham, 1839, from the Society for the Diffusion of Useful Knowledge (SDUK). (Bottom right segment)

Ten
CLEARING THE FROGGARY

L ondon publisher John Tallis issued his *Illustrated Atlas* in 1850, which consisted of eighty highly decorative maps of the countries and regions of the world, engraved on steel by John Rapkin. They are delicately engraved and are surrounded by charming vignettes depicting famous landmarks, wildlife and costume of the inhabitants of each country. By this time the accuracy and practicality of maps were generally considered of greater importance than aesthetic qualities, therefore making Tallis maps unusual for the period.

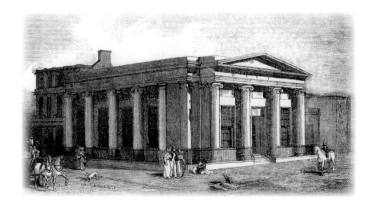

The news rooms.

Tallis did not produce a series of county maps, but his maps of the individual countries of the British Isles are well worthy of note. Between 1850 and 1860, Tallis published an extremely attractive series of town plans, also engraved by Rapkin, with vignettes of scenes and buildings taken from Thomas Dugdale's *Curiosities of Great Britain* (first published around 1835). Significantly, these plans include the rapidly expanding town of Birmingham during the Industrial Revolution.

By the mid-1800s Birmingham had other industrial rivals such as Manchester, but the trump card that would one day see Birmingham become Britain's second largest city was its extraordinarily varied industrial base. Birmingham had become the world's leading manufacturer of metal ware, but a wide range of other goods were also made. Businesses included brass, toy, button, jewellery, gun, pin, steel pen manufacture, coin and medal-making as well as the new electroplating process, flint glass and papier-mâché. Trades recorded in the 1851 census chronicled the large number of brass founders, gunsmiths, gold and silversmiths, button makers and tool makers who were employed in the town.

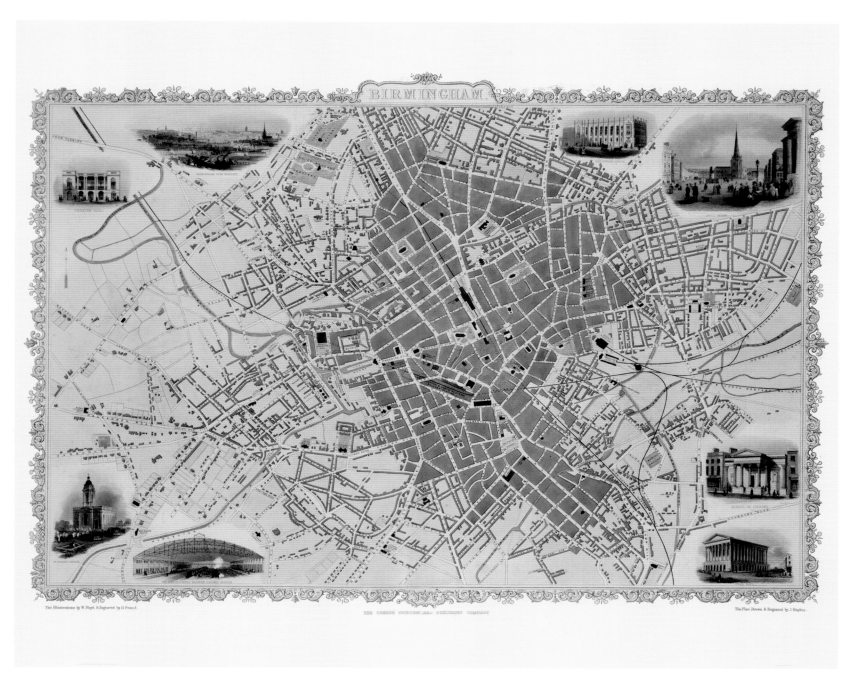

Plan of Birmingham, 1851, published by John Tallis, drawn and engraved by John Rapkin.

As Birmingham expanded out into the countryside, those people in the town centre were about to see great change. Despite the town's industrial progress, the quality of life for those living in the town would not really improve until the last quarter of the century. The catalyst for the change in the heart of Birmingham came in 1846 with the merger of the Grand Junction, the London and Birmingham, and Manchester and Birmingham railway companies. The newly formed London and North Western company was granted authority to extend its long awaited railway line about one mile from Curzon Street to the town centre at New Street. It was not just the railway company that would benefit; the town council seized the opportunity to try and improve one of its own problems – the lack of sewers.

In 1845 there were only around forty miles of sewers in Birmingham, all discharging straight into the River Rea or the Hockley Brook. Part of the agreement between the council and railway company involved the laying of sewage pipes in the centre of Birmingham at the railway company's expense.

Old prison,
Peck Lane.

At this early stage it is important to note that 'sewers' or 'sewage pipes' were used as a method of disposing of the town's excess water so as to prevent flooding. Sewage pipes were not built for the purpose of disposing of the town's sewage, which would include human excreta, as they are today. The increasing seepage into sewers of such matter (and contamination of water wells) from the many cesspits and often overflowing middens would create greater problems for the people of Birmingham as the century progressed.

In 1849 the town engineer, Robert Rawlinson, reported on the sanitary condition of Birmingham. He made recommendations for improving the housing of the working class, paving of streets, sewage disposal and uniform standard of clean cheap water. The latter two recommendations were to be placed under one sanitary authority. In 1851, with the passing of the Birmingham Improvement Act, the town could now raise loans for street and sewage improvements and the paving and cleaning of streets.

The first meeting of the Committee of Public Works took place on 2 January 1852. Mr John Piggott Smith was appointed Surveyor of the Borough with an annual salary of £600, together with the keep of two horses. (Earlier, in 1847, Piggott Smith produced a detailed plan of Birmingham; such is the scale that it consists of four large sheet sections.) Mr James Bliss was appointed Inspector of Nuisances with a salary of £150 per year. In the first year a private contractor took up the task of collecting the town's night soil (human waste) from outdoor privies, middens and dunghills for £4,200, but it soon came back under the jurisdiction of the Committee.

In 1847 a deal was struck with the railway company and the town council, and the enormous project

View across Birmingham in 1860, showing an early steam train approaching Birmingham across the bridge.

commenced. It would see the railway pass through to the heart of the town terminating at New Street, in what would be, albeit for a short time, one of the finest stations of its time. Central areas of the town would change forever, affecting both the living and the dead.

Work commenced on a one-mile deep open trench being dug, after land had been acquired, through to the station location. Buildings in the unsavoury 'Froggary', a network of courts and alleys, were demolished. Peck Lane, Colmore Street and King Street disappeared in the process. Religious buildings were also demolished; their graves being re-located elsewhere.

Another building of significant note would be demolished, although not many tears were shed on its demise. The prison on the corner of Pinfold Street and Peck Lane consisted of two cells and a courtyard of 25sq.ft. There were times when up to 100 prisoners were crammed in this dark, foreboding place.

The cost of pulling down and clearing buildings, and any other obstructions, exceeded £500,000 – an enormous sum for the time. In 1851 the railway had reached its destination with the opening of a temporary terminus at New Street. The process of transforming the terminus into the New Grand Central Railway Station did not take long; however, the official opening of the station did not take place until 1 June 1854. This coincided with the opening of the splendid frontage; the Queens Hotel. One of the vignette views on the plan by Tallis captures the inside of the station, showing the magnificent glass roof. At the time, and for the next fourteen years, it would have the largest iron and glass roof in the world, with a width of 212ft and 840ft in length. In the same year the Midland Railway trains that had used Curzon Street switched to New Street.

Tallis shows the well-developed railway system, the routes and recently constructed tunnels made using the 'cut and cover' method, rather than tunnelling. Not far from New Street Station is the rival railway company, the Great Western Railway Company. The station at Snow Hill at this time was a large wooden shed, named at the time of the plan as Livery Street Station, built on the ground formally occupied by a large glass works. It would not be named Snow Hill Station until 1858.

Birmingham's trade and industry would benefit enormously from the railways – we had already moved to an era where destination would be measured by time and not distance. The country's capital was now under three hours away.

Queens Hotel frontage to New Street Station, 1854.

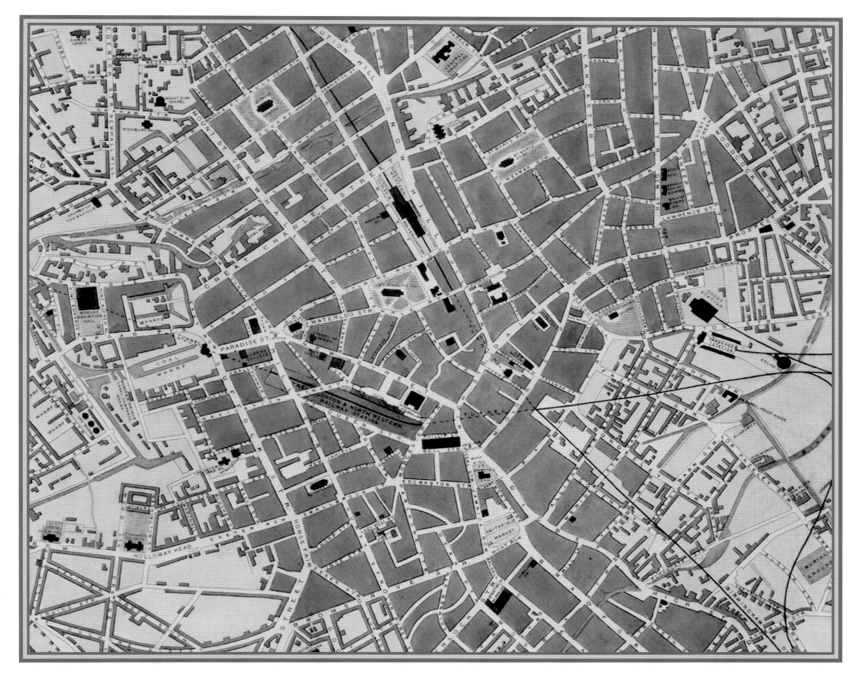

Plan of Birmingham, 1851, published by John Tallis, drawn and engraved by John Rapkin. (Middle segment)

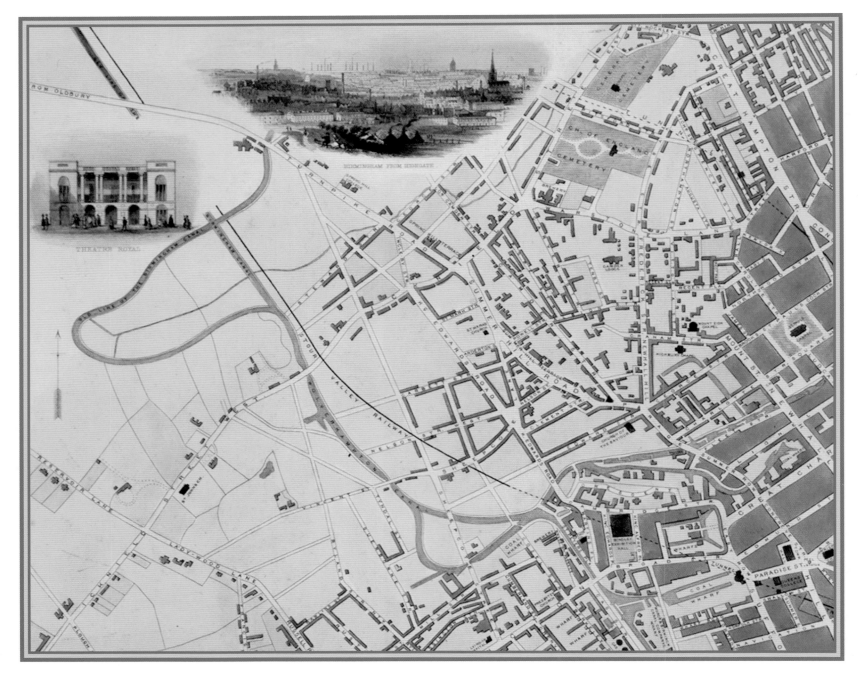

Plan of Birmingham, 1851, published by John Tallis, drawn and engraved by John Rapkin. (Top left segment)

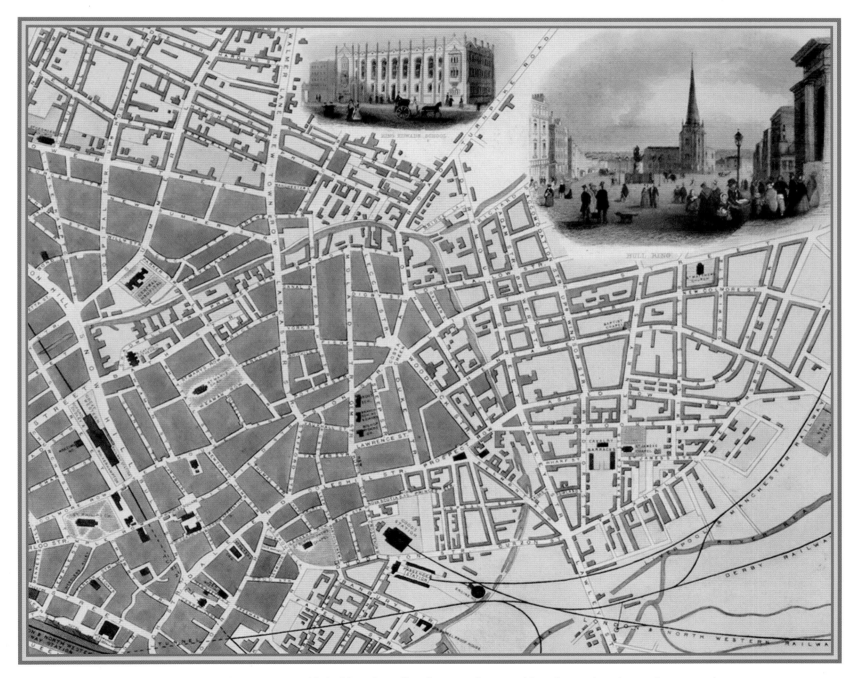

Plan of Birmingham, 1851, published by John Tallis, drawn and engraved by John Rapkin. (Top right segment)

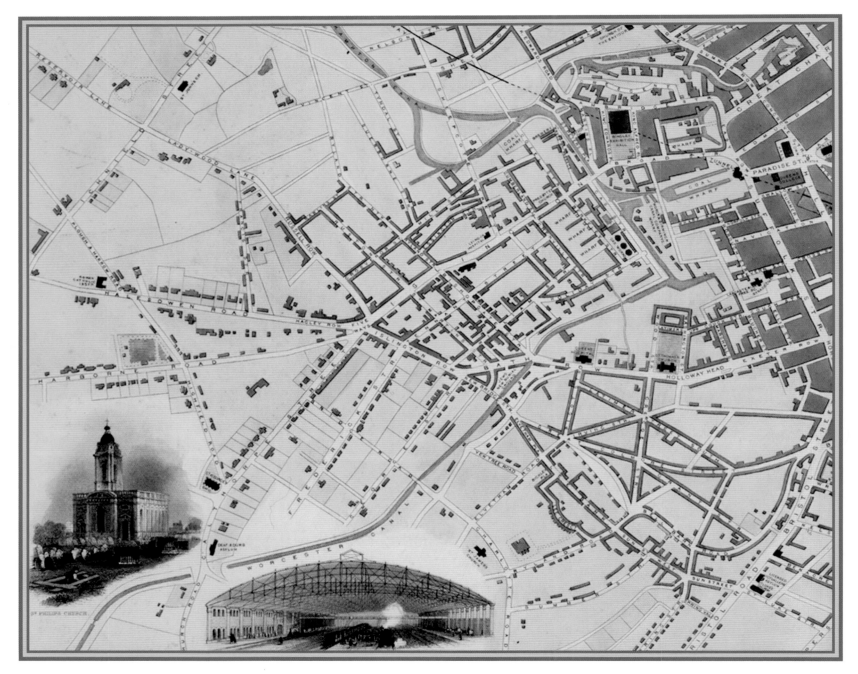

Plan of Birmingham, 1851, published by John Tallis, drawn and engraved by John Rapkin. (Bottom left segment)

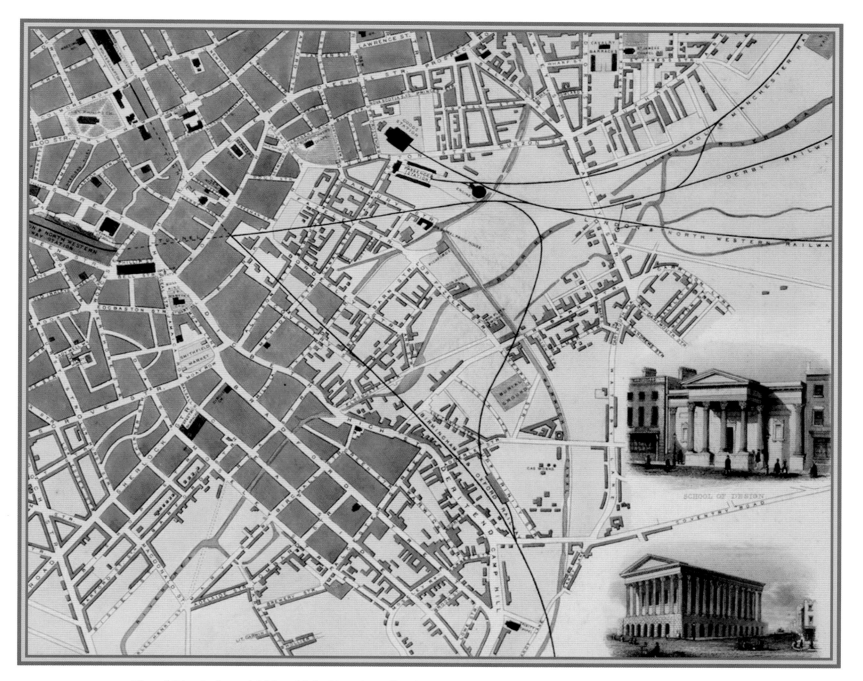

Plan of Birmingham, 1851, published by John Tallis, drawn and engraved by John Rapkin. (Bottom right segment)

Eleven
GREEN OPEN SPACES

Archibald Fullarton was a well known publisher of books in the nineteenth century; however, it is of significant note that the engraver, John Bartholomew Junior, had followed in the footsteps of his father and grandfather, establishing the reputation of the famous Bartholomew map-making company based in Edinburgh, Scotland. John Bartholomew Junior was the first person to use layer colouring to indicate land heights and sea depths. The Bartholomew map-making generations would continue to prosper by introducing new map-making techniques well into the twentieth century; it is a name synonymous with maps, plans and surveys to this very day.

The plan of 1866 covers a greater area than all previous plans, stretching out to include Aston – a district as yet not incorporated into Birmingham. To the south there is Edgbaston; the small village of Harborne is also just about featured. However, this plan reveals something new, something that Birmingham's inhabitants had needed for quite some time – public open space. The green-coloured areas add a splash of colour to the plan, highlighting the arrival of Birmingham's first parks.

The desperate need for expanses of open space for those living in rapidly growing towns like Birmingham was recognised by the early years of the nineteenth century. Unfortunately it did not become a reality until the 1840s, when the first public parks were opened in Derby and Manchester. Birmingham was not far behind when it opened its first park in 1856.

Adderley Park is on the right of the plan. Charles Adderley, later first Lord Norton, owned much of the area around Duddeston and Vauxhall; he donated land

Summerfield House on Birmingham Heath.

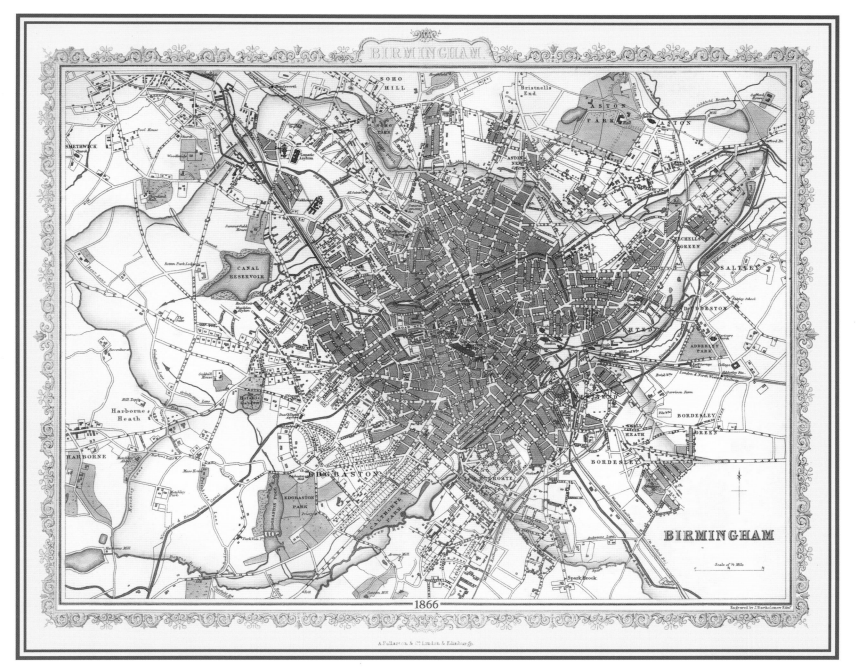

Plan of Birmingham, 1866, published by Archibald Fullarton & Co., engraved by J. Bartholomew.

for Birmingham's first park. Calthorpe Park, hugging the banks of the River Rea to the south, was opened a year later on 1 June 1857 by the Duke of Cambridge, in the presence of around 100,000 people. The park was a gift from Lord Calthorpe.

Other features of note on the plan include the canal reservoir, which was built in 1827 by Thomas Telford to top up Birmingham's canal system. Birmingham's Botanical Gardens opened in 1832 and was becoming an important attraction. Soho Park and Soho Pool (formally the Great Hockley Pool) would soon disappear, as with Matthew Boulton's Soho Manufactory towards the end of the 1840s. Fortunately, his former residence, which overlooked the manufactory and park, is still here today for all those who wish to explore the life of Birmingham's most famous industrialist.

While the introduction of public parks heralded some relief, living conditions in the town had worsened. One of the first major changes designed to improve living conditions would be the effective improvement in the town's water supply. This would be brought about by the removal of sources of pollution from the many local wells and pumps used to draw water in Birmingham.

The pressure on the Corporation of Birmingham to bring about this change was not as a result of the many medical reports that recorded misery, disease and an appalling death rate amongst young children. Instead, following consistent breaches of court injunctions prohibiting Birmingham Council from polluting the river Tame and its tributaries, Birmingham had no choice but to find a way of keeping its excreta, which eventually found its way into the River Rea and Tame, out of the sewers.

In 1871 a special committee was formed to consider and report on the best method of dealing with Birmingham's sewage. After visiting other towns the committee concluded that the necessary sanitary improvements required could be effected either by the introduction of a water closet system, as used in Liverpool, or a privy system as adopted in Rochdale and Manchester. Unlike Liverpool, Birmingham did not have an abundant supply of water. Therefore the committee concluded that it should gradually carry out the abolition of middens, replacing them with the privy system. There would be weekly collections of excreta in an attempt to keep it from any other sewage matter.

In 1874 the 'Rochdale Pan Method' (a removable receptacle under the closet seat) was finally introduced into Birmingham, after the acquisition of pans, carts and cleaning equipment. Once a week the night soil men collected pans and tubs for ashes, taking them to the corporation wharf in Montague Street. With the adoption of the pan system, and the removal of Birmingham's middens, the immediate problem from the vicinity of the local wells improved as the seepage from pollution into them, as well as nearby sewers, was removed.

In 1875 the Birmingham Water Works company was transferred to the Corporation and water supply into the town gradually improved. With an increased water supply the method became uneconomical by 1888, and water closets were gradually introduced. In 1893 the Elan Valley project commenced – an abundant supply of fresh water would soon be flowing, all the way from Wales.

Night soil van.

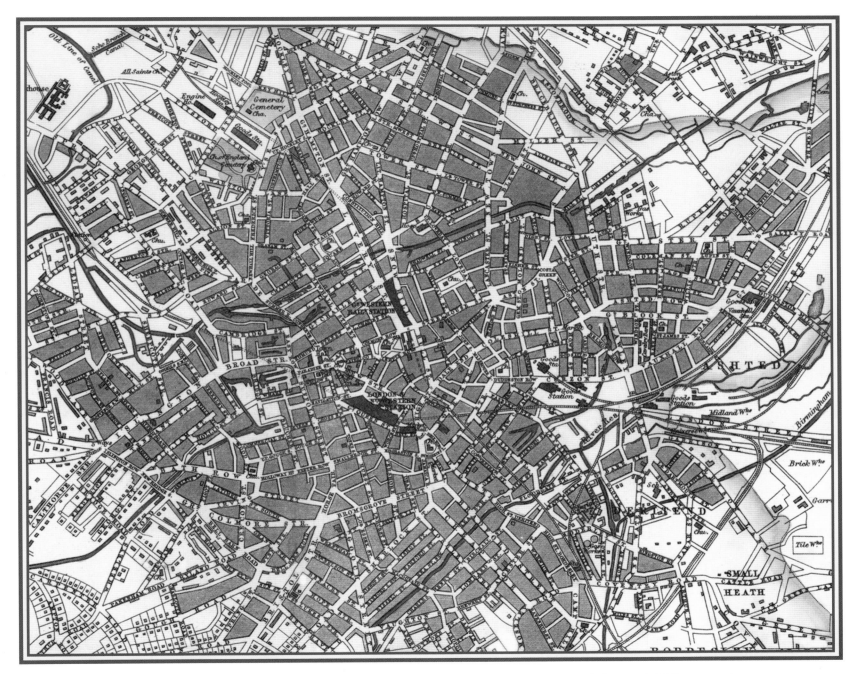

Plan of Birmingham, 1866, published by Archibald Fullarton & Co., engraved by J. Bartholomew. (Middle segment)

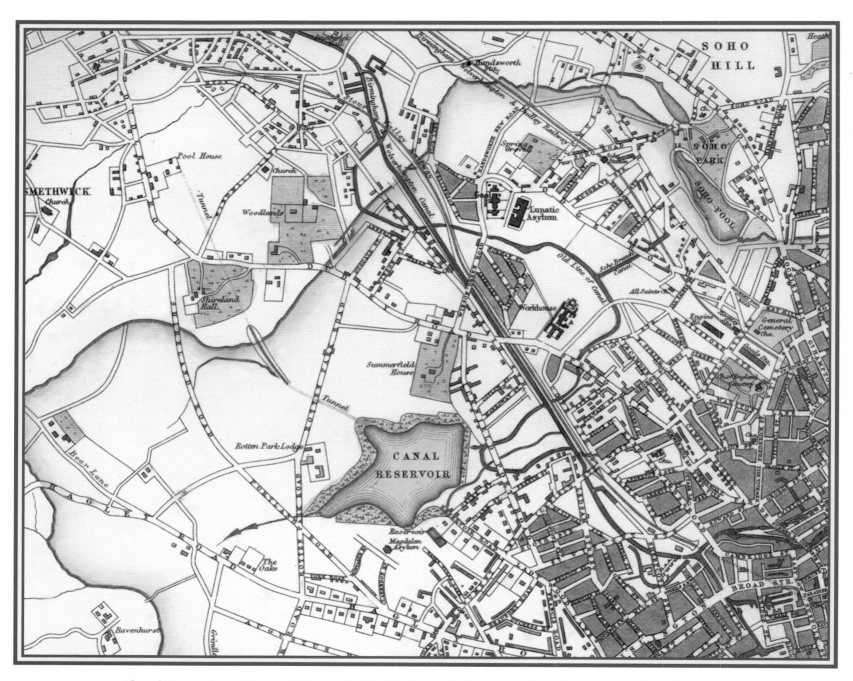

Plan of Birmingham, 1866, published by Archibald Fullarton & Co., engraved by J. Bartholomew. (Top left segment)

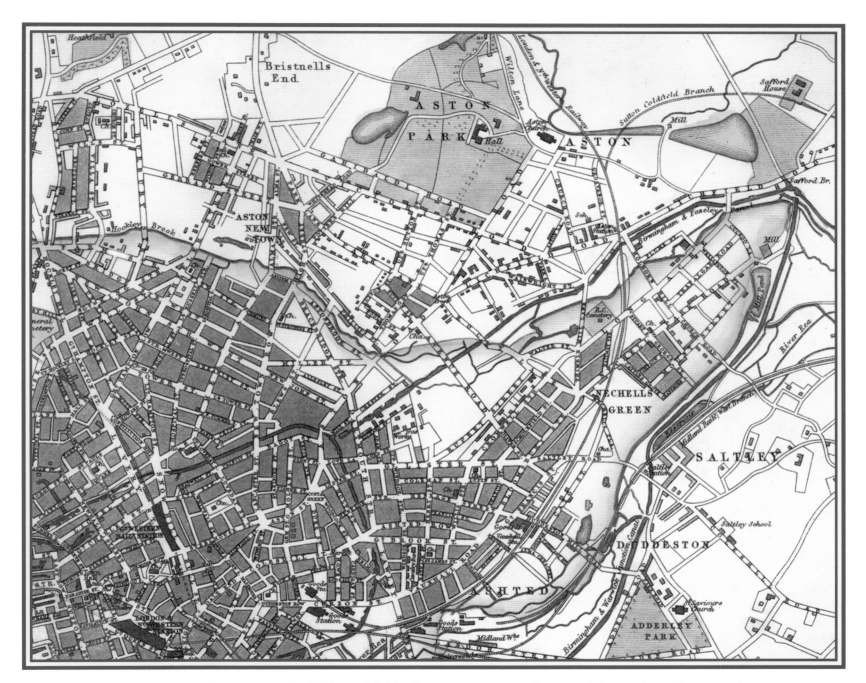

Plan of Birmingham, 1866, published by Archibald Fullarton & Co., engraved by J. Bartholomew. (Top right segment)

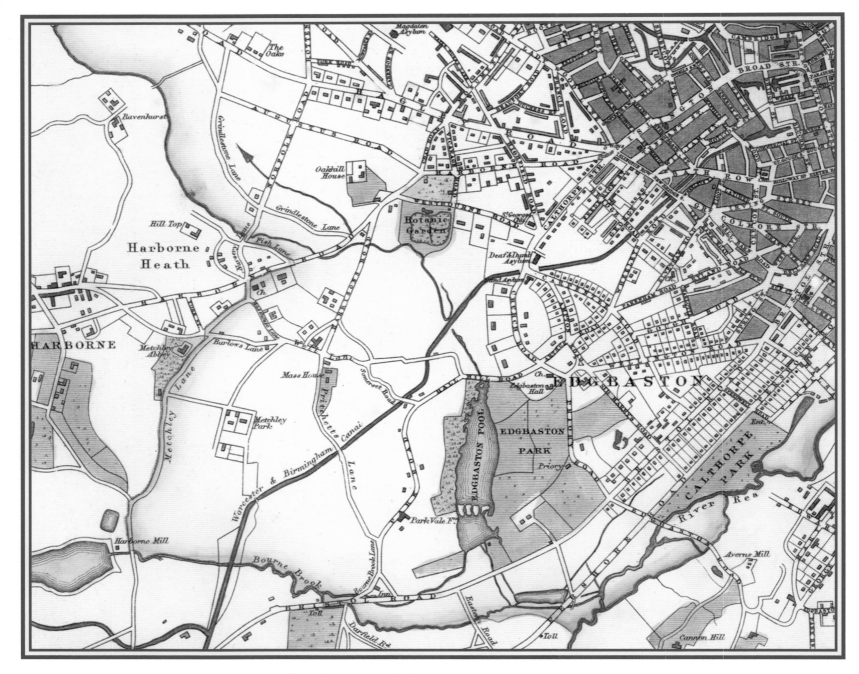

Plan of Birmingham, 1866, published by Archibald Fullarton & Co., engraved by J. Bartholomew. (Bottom left segment)

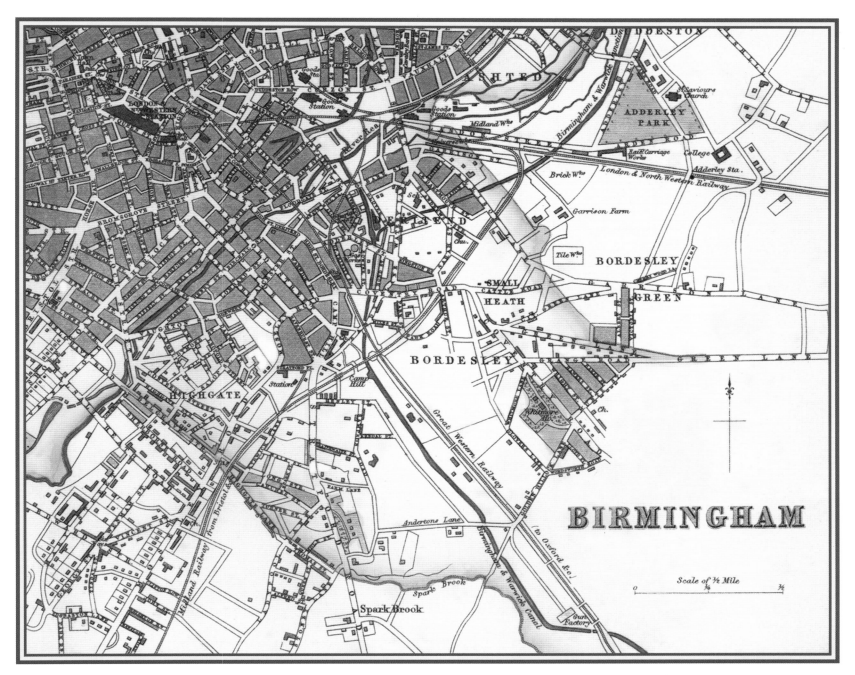

Plan of Birmingham, 1866, published by Archibald Fullarton & Co., engraved by J. Bartholomew. (Bottom right segment)

Twelve

VISIONARY LEADERS AND SPORTING PIONEERS

The plan of Birmingham 1893 (opposite) is one of many town plans contained within a six volume, comprehensive and highly detailed resource covering England and Wales. Information contained within was based on the tenth census of 1891. The maps of the counties were specially reduced from the Ordnance Survey by Mr F.S. Weller, FRGS. The work was collated by an experienced team of compilers under the editorship of Mr J.H.F. Brabner, FRGS.

Offices of the bank of Birmingham, Bennett's Hill.

Queen Victoria granted Birmingham city status in 1889. It was by now the largest and most important industrial centre in the country. The city had spread north to Aston and was reaching out to Harborne. Harborne, Balsall Heath, Saltley and Little Bromwich were brought into the city in 1891. Factory chimneys dominated the smoke-filled skyline, where a multitude of trades poured out their wares for distribution both nationally and internationally.

In the second half of the nineteenth century, Birmingham's political elite finally began to take notice of the terrible conditions affecting the poor of the city; many were living in squalid conditions in the slum areas of Birmingham. When Joseph Chamberlain became mayor of Birmingham in 1873, he led a dynamic and pro-active team that transformed many areas in the centre of the city that had degenerated into a labyrinth of crime and squalor, the principal area being the old Priory Estate. Chamberlain's 'Improvement Scheme' was made possible by the passing of the Artisans' Dwelling Act in 1875. This Act gave them permission to purchase unsanitary areas within the town borders, demolish

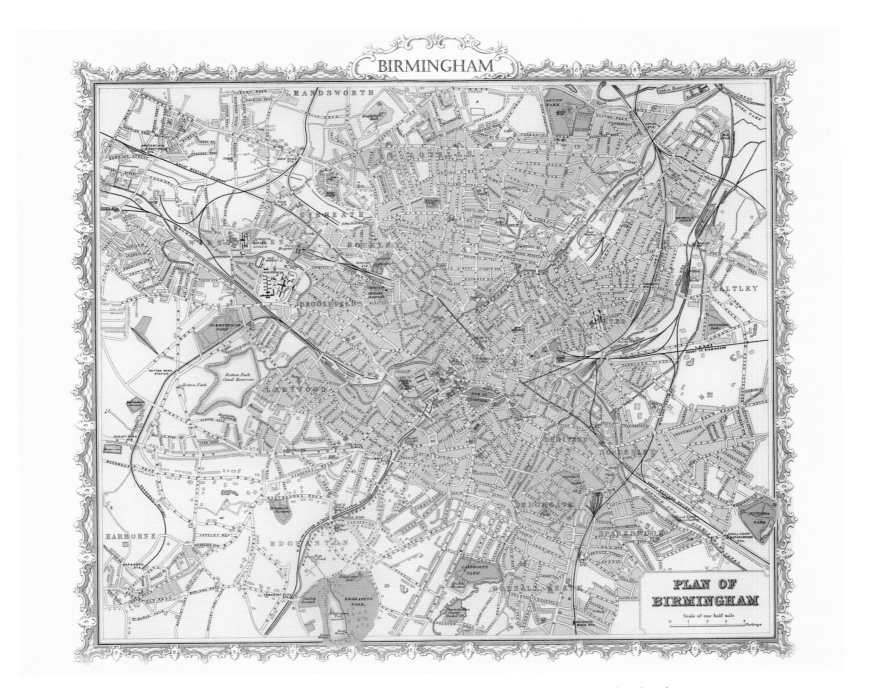

Street plan of Birmingham, 1893, from the Comprehensive Gazetteer of England and Wales.

buildings unsuitable for habitation and construct new buildings to replace them.

Many of the old Georgian houses were pulled down, and large tracts of slum areas were demolished, with new streets being cut with rows of imposing Victorian buildings. Of the new streets to appear, namely John Bright Street, Martineau Street and Corporation Street, the latter embellished a new cosmopolitan image that would be Chamberlain's legacy. His administration was ultimately responsible for the provision of gas, municipalisation of the water supply, development of sewerage systems and increase in the number of boarding schools now required in Birmingham.

Chamberlain was a supporter of the Elementary Education Act of 1870 (also known as Forster's Education Act). This set the framework for the schooling of all children between the ages of five and twelve. Like the rest of the country, in 1884 all Birmingham children were required to attend school up to the age of twelve.

After the Whigs gained power in Parliament, the Ten Hour Bill (also known as the Ten Hour Act) was passed, becoming the Factories Act 1847. This law limited the working week in textile mills for women and children under eighteen years of age. In effect, this law limited the workday to ten hours. It limited the hours of labour to sixty-three per week from 1 July 1847, and to fifty-eight per week from 1 May 1848, which, with the stoppage on Saturday afternoon, was the equivalent of ten hours work per day.

Leisure time was important in an age when religious conformity was strict and the *beau ideal* of healthy Christianity in Victorian England was encouraged through athletic pastimes and games.

The 'gentleman's' game of cricket was by now a popular sporting pastime. The plan of 1893 is the first to show Warwickshire County Cricket Ground. History led to Birmingham, not Leamington near Warwick, being chosen as the home of the Midland County Club. The land was made fit for the purpose and the first game played in 1886.

As for the game of association football, the plan is too early to show the famous grounds of the two clubs who would go on to become the second city rivals of today. However, they were already well established, and very successful. By now, each Saturday afternoon during the winter months, a fair cross-section of Birmingham society would support their favourite team. Well-to-do businessmen and iron masters often stood shoulder-to-shoulder with grimy Black Country puddlers, tough Birmingham foundrymen in their filthy moleskins, and a sprinkling of high-collared office workers. But they could all raise a cheer together when the 'Perry Barr Pets' (Aston Villa, then based at Perry Barr) or the 'Alliance' (Small Heath Alliance, later Birmingham City) were on the attack.

The beginnings of these longstanding football clubs date back to the first half of the1870s, when Birmingham, with sinewy arms and sooty face, was continuing to forge its name in brass and iron as the workshop of the world. It was back then when a few young cricketers stroked their whiskers and thought seriously of taking up the new game so that they could remain together and maintain their fitness during the winter ready for summer cricket.

As the new century dawned, the Victorian age bid farewell. During the last decade a number of prominent buildings were built as lasting icons to that great era; the Victoria Law Courts, Birmingham Museum and Art Gallery being fine examples. It would also herald the arrival of the motor car. Its effect on the prevalent mode of transport in the Victorian age, the railway, would be significant. Its impact on Birmingham, Britain, and the rest of the world, would be far greater.

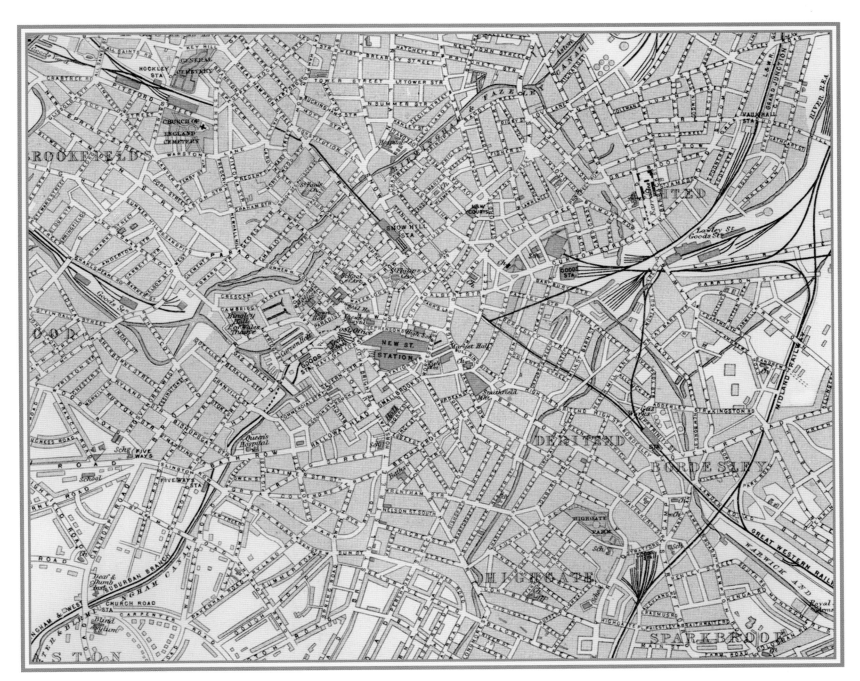

Street plan of Birmingham, 1893, from the Comprehensive Gazetteer of England and Wales. *(Middle segment)*

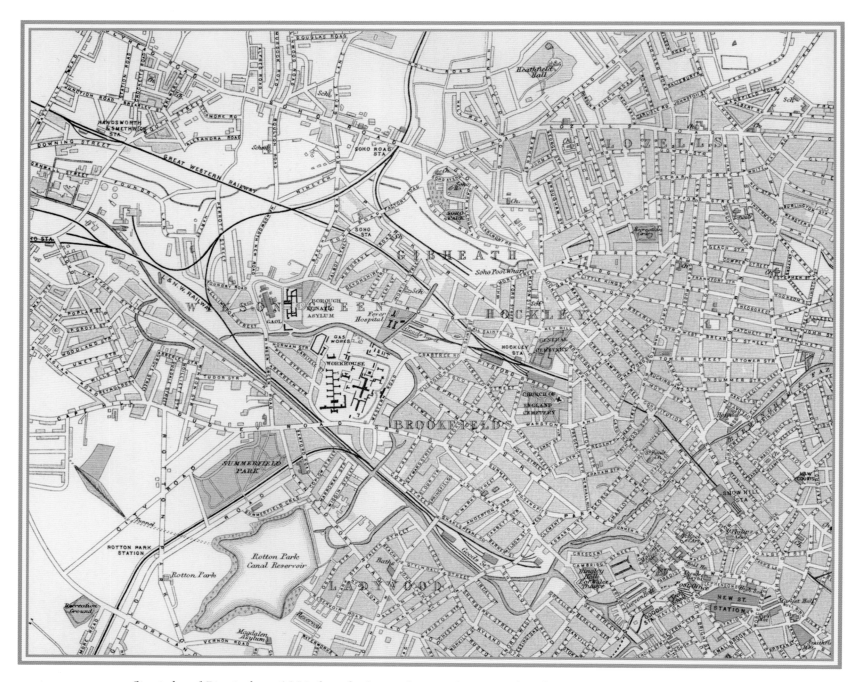

Street plan of Birmingham, 1893, from the Comprehensive Gazetteer of England and Wales. *(Top left segment)*

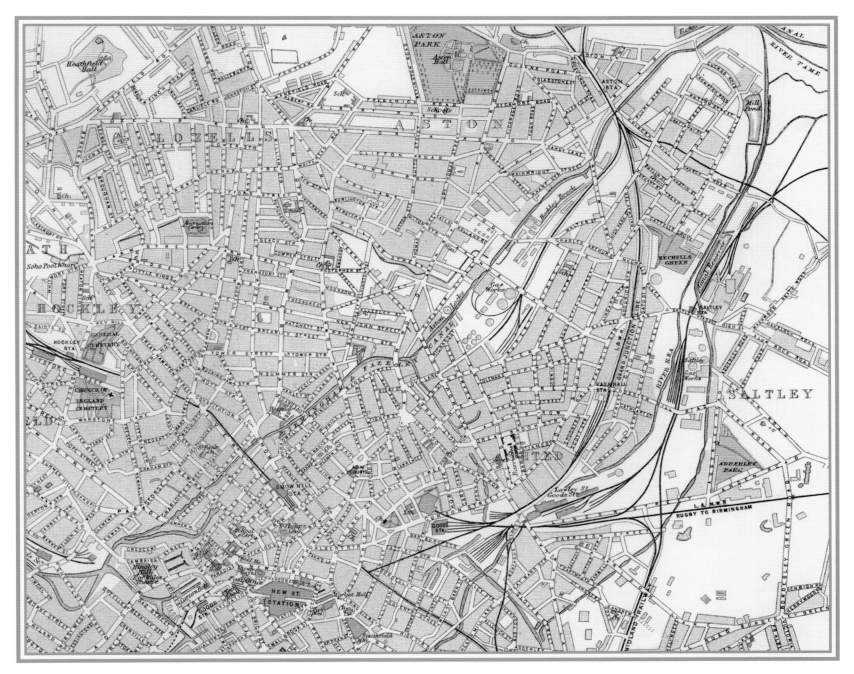

Street plan of Birmingham, 1893, from the Comprehensive Gazetteer of England and Wales. *(Top right segment)*

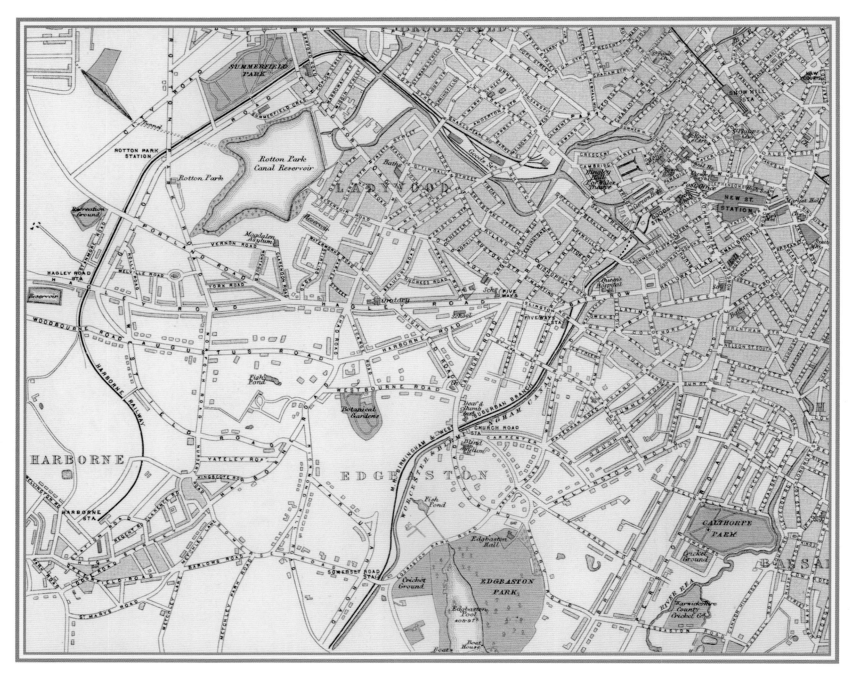

Street plan of Birmingham, 1893, from the Comprehensive Gazetteer of England and Wales. *(Bottom left segment)*

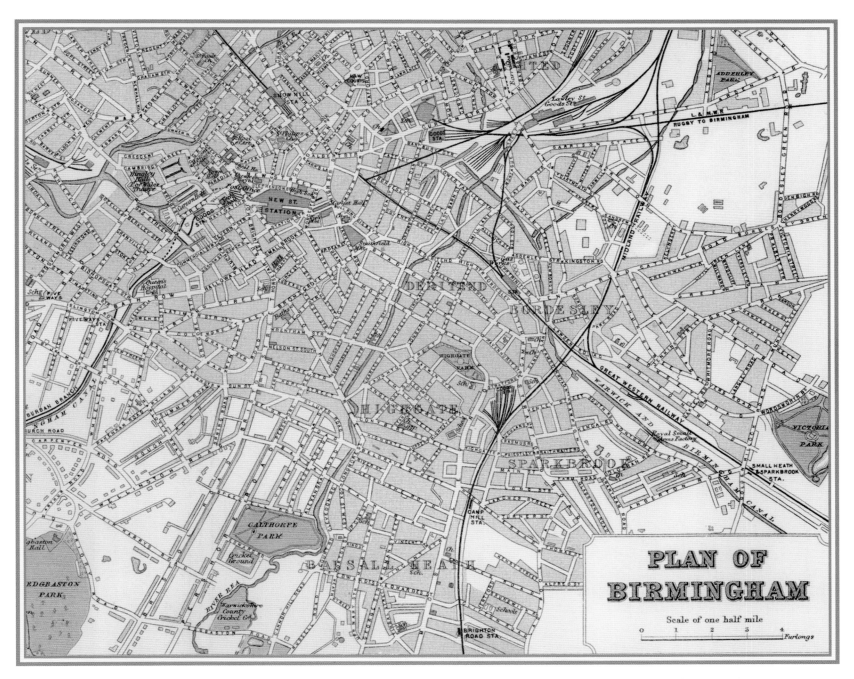

Street plan of Birmingham, 1893, from the Comprehensive Gazetteer of England and Wales. *(Bottom right segment)*

Thirteen

THE MOTOR CAR AND 'MOTOR CITY'

Birmingham Museum and Art Gallery.

Illustrated opposite is a section from the 'AA Duplex Throughway Map of Birmingham'. The original was produced on a scale of 2.65 inches to the mile and shows streets, throughways, public buildings, public houses, golf courses, car parks etc. The original displays a fully detailed map of Birmingham's surrounding country (with contour colouring on the reverse side), that was being consumed somewhat further by the city as the century progressed. The map was published by John Bartholomew & Son Ltd in August 1949 on Manila paper and cost 7s and 6d. The map was revised at frequent intervals, the road revision being carried out by the Automobile Association.

The Bartholomew company was involved in supporting Britain's war effort by producing maps, plans and surveys. The post-war years saw the prolific map-making company returning to commercial map publishing on a scale that could not have been imagined just a few years previously. By the late 1940s and '50s the number of motorists on Britain's, and indeed on Birmingham's, roads was growing rapidly and motoring maps and atlases were purchased in large numbers. These good times were made even better by the growing number of people escaping to the country at weekends to cycle and walk, who required detailed maps.

After emerging from two world wars, the importance of Birmingham's great contribution and the heavy price paid for its vital industrial capacity should not be underestimated. During the First World War, Birmingham sent 150,000 men and boys to the trenches of Europe; many did not return. Its many factories produced equipment from machine guns to armoured vehicles and poured out millions of cartridges and shells.

During the Second World War the Luftwaffe failed to break the morale of Birmingham's workers and destroy its priceless industry. Around 400,000 of the city's population were engaged in war production.

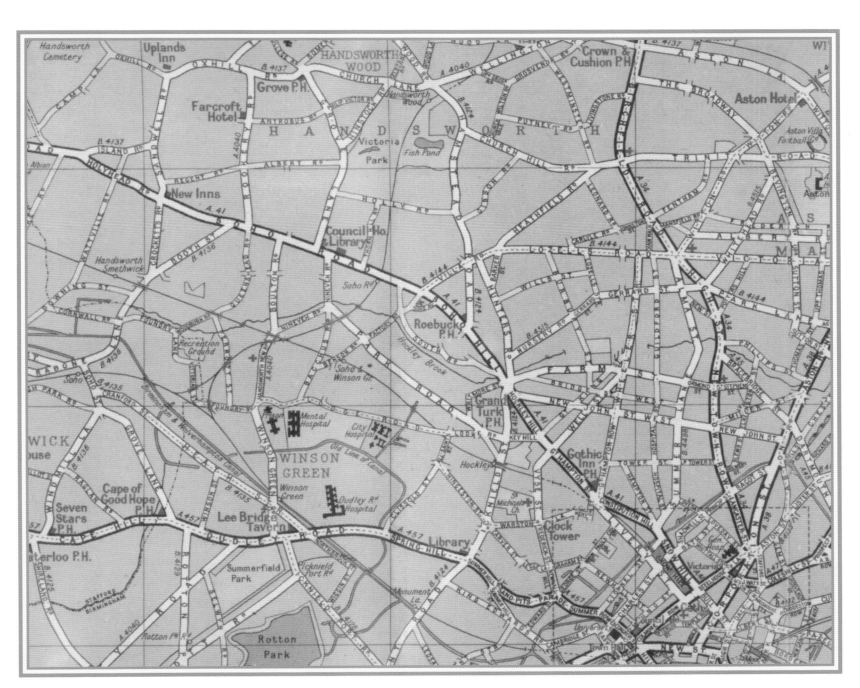

AA Duplex Throughway Map of Birmingham, 1949, published by John Bartholomew & Son Ltd. (Top left segment)

As well as manufacturing ammunition, shells, fighting vehicles, engine components, motorcycles, trucks and much more, now with Spitfires and Hurricanes flowing out of Birmingham's factories it was a prime target for the German command. During the Blitz, 5,000 citizens would be killed or injured, over 6,000 homes reduced to rubble, and many characteristically outstanding buildings lost or seriously damaged.

It was the time for re-building. However, it has been said that the city of Birmingham was partly destroyed by German bombing during the war, but completely destroyed by council concrete redevelopment in the 1960s.

As with many old maps, plans or surveys, it is easy to get drawn into their many facets of detail. I am sure that the 1949 street plan will bring back fond memories for many people today. The BSA factory, the Singer factory, and perhaps a number of public houses that have now disappeared or been converted to fast food and buffet restaurants, leave many Birmingham people feeling nostalgic.

The plan of 1949 is an example from which we can graphically look at Birmingham for the last time before

The new Bull Ring shopping centre.

many street connections lined with fine buildings were lost. The concept of the walking street was soon to be replaced with the concept of the individual building accessed by car from the engineered highway.

This transition took place in the 1950s and '60s, changing Birmingham from an historical and traditional city of streets into a 'motor city'. The inner ring road was built, forming a tight concrete collar around the heart of the city that included historic markets and a distinctive array of public squares. A direct motorway link to the city centre would be a first for Birmingham; the scheme to build the Aston Expressway was under the condition that it would be ready for the new and complex M6 Interchange at Gravelly Hill in 1972. This was achieved and Birmingham was soon associated with 'Spaghetti Junction'.

During the 1960s great change was to occur at the heart of the city that would see in two new Birmingham icons, and see the burial of a former. The market site was developed, creating at the time one of the world's largest enclosed shopping centres – the Bull Ring, and the Rotunda opened in 1965. After sustaining bomb damage, the glass roof of New Street Station was taken down between 1948 and 1952; its imposing frontage, the Queens Hotel, was demolished. The former great station was then buried under shopping centres and car parks.

Birmingham's world-renowned Bull Ring shopping centre opened in 2003 and has been cited as the catalyst for Birmingham's future regeneration. Drawing on Birmingham's traditional and historic street patterns, it now provides a gateway to Eastside, where plans have commenced to create 'City Park', one of several major projects revitalising the greater city of Birmingham by extending the network of squares, spaces and streets out from its centre – for the people.

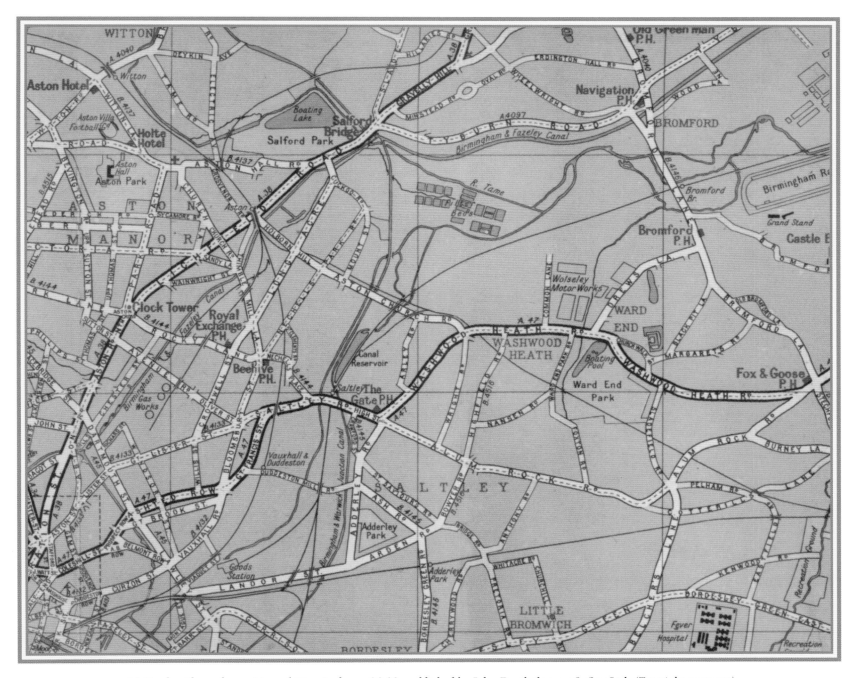

AA Duplex Throughway Map of Birmingham, 1949, published by John Bartholomew & Son Ltd. (Top right segment)

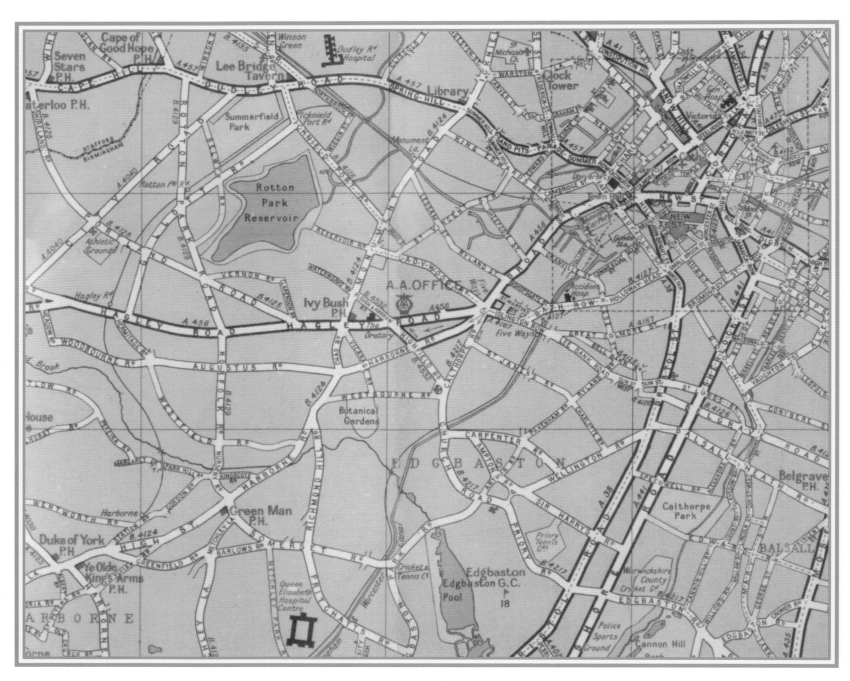

AA Duplex Throughway Map of Birmingham, 1949, published by John Bartholomew & Son Ltd. (Bottom left segment)

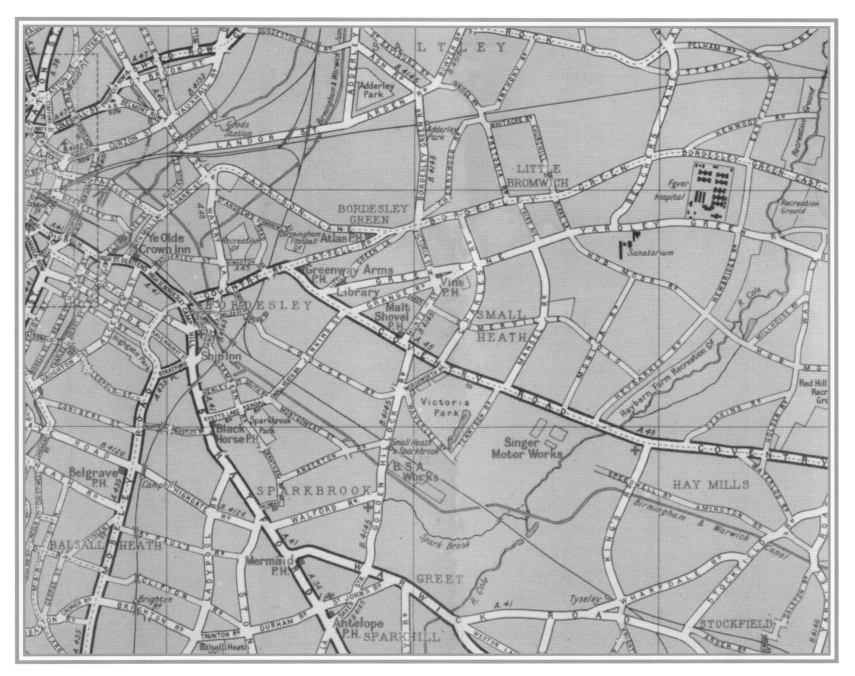

AA Duplex Throughway Map of Birmingham, 1949, published by John Bartholomew & Son Ltd. (Bottom right segment)

Fourteen

BIRMINGHAM: THE FUTURE VISION

As I looked out across Birmingham from the top of Alpha Tower, the city spread out 360 degrees around me; a sprawling mass of mixed conurbation stretching out into the distance as far as the eye can see. What the thoughts of Westley, Hanson and Kempson would be if they could see the same view of Birmingham that I can see today, we can only imagine.

Our historic and listed buildings have a special place in the future vision; not to be overshadowed, but to

A futuristic vision of historic Curzon Street Station, facing City Park, 2013. The image shows part of the 1.4m sq.ft proposed 'Curzon Street' mixed use redevelopment scheme, a joint venture between Development Securities Plc and Grainger Plc.

stand out and be part of the future. We must find them that special place and that special purpose. We must learn from the lessons of the past, particularly from the 1960s, when we suffered from short and narrow vision, at the cost of our heritage.

We have lost many industries that made Birmingham what it is today; we have also lost many historic buildings. But maybe the worst loss has been the steady degeneration of the very infrastructure around the city core, those districts effectively that are in between the city centre and the ring road.

Not many decades ago our aging and neglected canals, which first brought the life blood of transport through its many arteries, were responsible for further decay of areas of land adjacent to the endless towpaths. After much thought, investment and future planning, we have re-created the canals for a different purpose; now they attract people, enable social interaction of communities and promote continued investment. The canals have now become part of Birmingham's leisure metropolis.

We cannot bring back the many grand buildings that were bulldozed when Birmingham was transformed into a 'Motor City'. At the same time, the good street connections across the town were lost when the concrete collar, the ring road, was constructed. However, these unique districts can be transformed and revitalised by connecting them once again with the heart of the city itself, adopting a similar train of thought as with the canals.

In actually doing this, with a message similar to that of Chamberlain when he staked his vision in the nineteenth century, Birmingham's planners have embarked on a most ambitious and far-reaching citywide development project, raising Birmingham's status once again, this time on a global scale.

Artist's impression of Birmingham, 2013 – City Park, Eastland.

PICTURE CREDITS

St Martin's Church in the Bull Ring, 2009.